Foundations

Preparing the Church in Australia for the Plenary Council and beyond

Everyone then who hears these words of mine and does them will be like a wise man who built his house upon the rock.
Mt 7:24

Julian Porteous

Connor Court Publishing Pty Ltd

Connor Court Publishing Pty Ltd

Copyright © Julian Porteous 2021

ALL RIGHTS RESERVED. This book contains material protected under International and Federal Copyright Laws and Treaties. Any unauthorised reprint or use of this material is prohibited. No part of this book may be reproduced or transmitted in any form or by any means, electronic or mechanical, including photocopying, recording, or by any information storage and retrieval system without express written permission from the publisher.
PO Box 7257
Redland Bay QLD 4165
sales@connorcourt.com
www.connorcourt.com

ISBN: 9781922449658

Cover design by Maria Giordano

Printed in Australia

To St Joseph, Patron of the Universal Church,
in this Year of St Joseph, 2021

Contents

Foreword	vii
1. Reading the Times	1
2. Christ – The Foundation	7
3. The Cultural Shift	21
4. Rebuilding a Culture of Catholic Marriage and Family	35
5. A Renewal in Catechesis	51
6. Understanding the Nature of the Church	63
7. The Pastoral Challenge	73
8. The Parish, a Missionary Focused Community	81
9. Signs of Hope	95

Foreword

The forthcoming Plenary Council offers an unusual opportunity for Australian Catholics to strengthen the Church's foundations as Archbishop Julian desires, when bishops, laity, clergy and religious gather for discussion and decision. We pray that they will listen to the Word of God in the Scriptures.

All will be prayerful people of good-will, but success is not guaranteed, however it may be defined. Doctrinal, theological and pastoral positions might be irreconcilable and consequent disappointment could even be tinged with bitterness, especially if initial expectations are unrealistic, envisaging impossibilities.

Recently (April 2021), Cardinal Pietro Parolin, Secretary of State, was pointing out that sometimes Catholics are confused over the hierarchy of truths, over what doctrines are central and essential and therefore cannot be abandoned; over theological differences where a pluralism is acceptable and even over pastoral and liturgical practices which can be various.

The Council will be a national Catholic gathering, representing a small vital community of 5.5 million believers in a world-wide communion of 1.33 billion baptised Catholics. The worship, prayer and discussion will take place within the parameters developed during nearly 2000 years of tradition in a single Church, led by the Holy Father, now Pope Francis, the successor of Peter, the 'rock-man' on whom the Church is built (Mt 16:18), and the bishops who are the successors of the Apostles.

There is no such thing as the Catholic Church of Australia, but we certainly have a wonderful life-giving community of the baptised, where only a small percentage are clergy or religious. This community of service constitutes the Catholic Church in Australia.

Pope Benedict has stated baldly to his fellow Germans that the world does not need another Protestant Church; indeed this is not a Catholic option, and the emeritus pope would say the same to us.

We all understand that the Church cannot be completely inclusive, as those who do not believe in God, or do not believe that Jesus in the Son of God, or do not believe in the two great commandments of love and in the Ten Commandments received by Moses, cannot be baptised. A person who does not believe in sin, rejects the need for repentance and conversion, who believes only in the certainty of death, but not in Heaven, Hell and Divine Judgement, should not seek to enter the Church. Following Christ is hard and costly; each has to take up his cross (Mk 8:34).

Local Councils and Synods have been a feature of some periods of Church history, but not all, as such gatherings are always imperfect, even frustrating, but often valuable. Over the centuries, these synods have dealt with many different problems in many different ways. However, the Church has only one set of doctrines, defined by the Magisterium and set out classically in the creeds and the rules of faith. Neither can there be any Australian version of the ten commandments.

All Catholics, from pope to the newly-baptised stand under the same Word of God, under the Truth, and no one, including the Holy Father, has the power to reject what is revealed in the Scriptures and solemnly taught. As Catholics we are Gospel Christians, who believe the last word on any doctrine of faith and morals has to be rooted in the Apostolic Tradition, not in modern understandings which contradict the Apostolic Tradition.

Archbishop Porteous realises all this and is striving to spell out the fixed points as the assembly works and prays to discern the signs of the times. Fixed points, such as the established doctrines on the structure of the Church, on the ministerial priesthood reserved for men, and on moral issues about the beginning and the end of life, on marriage and family, and the importance of heteronormativity.

There is in this book an abundance of information and insight on our changing society and Church where the percentage of Sunday Mass-goers has declined spectacularly, but where the number of Catholics continued to increase until the last ten years and the provision of Catholic services in health, education, aged-care, and social welfare has increased significantly over the last fifty years – often with the help of government finance. The need for evangelisation and community building are stressed, so that the "intentional Catholics" can be a leaven in society and pass on the flame of faith to the next generations.

We hope and pray that the Council does not become just another discussion group, but sponsors renewal and specific programs. Two challenges come to mind quickly.

A national working group should be set up to defend the freedom of religion both nationally and in the states, culturally, politically and legally. Religious allies will be easily found for this purpose. Archbishop Porteous knows this problem first-hand and the bishops and the Council should rally the Catholic people to defend their freedom as they defended the Catholic schools successfully in the later nineteenth century against free, compulsory, and secular education.

The flood of pornography, especially on the internet, is already causing widespread damage across the generations, producing addicts, breaking families, and destroying patterns of natural sexual activity. A national Church response in the dioceses, similar perhaps to that in the United States, is needed to help those who are tempted and those who have been captured.

Many parts of Australia, not perhaps Tasmania, are short of water. People understand what we are claiming when we describe the Catholic tradition as a mighty river which has watered Australian society since European settlement.

Many of the forces hostile to the Church are also hostile to our way of life, to Western civilisation. When the concept of truth is denied, when due process and the rule of law are attacked by mobs in the press and on the social media, notions such as free speech, the importance of debate and discussion within a climate of tolerance and civility are themselves threatened. Our social capital is being diminished as our enemies try to silence Christian voices in the parliaments, the press and the media, in public life generally. We must keep talking.

As Australian Catholics gather in Council they should not turn in on themselves, but understand and accept their obligations to God, the future, and the wider society. They should, more than ever, ask the Holy Spirit to help all of us better serve the disadvantaged and marginalised. The Catholic Church in Australia is called to continue to be *Lumen Gentium*, the light of the nations (*LG* 1,1).

+**George Cardinal Pell**
Rome, 19 April 2021

1

READING THE TIMES

For any Catholic living in Australia at the present moment the challenges to the faith are great indeed. The culture around us is changing rapidly, not only abandoning its Christian heritage but becoming increasingly hostile to the Church. Within the Church there is a serious struggle to know how to respond to these changes. Does the Church adapt itself to the culture? How can it preserve its true identity?

The evident decline in religion and in numbers of Catholics attending Sunday Mass and living a sacramental life is another area of concern. Is this decline terminal? Experiences like the sexual abuse crisis have further eroded the confidence of many Catholics, and some have lost confidence in the leadership of bishops. Is it time to change the governance structures of the Church?

As the Church prepares for a Plenary Council, these and many other issues challenge the Church here in Australia. Will the Council find the right way forward and plot a course which will ensure that the Church is able to effectively carry out the mission entrusted to it by the Lord?

The response we make to the issues we face must be grounded in a deep spirit of faith. It must be faithful to the revelation of Sacred

Scripture. It must be grounded in its living Tradition, and continuous with the body of Magisterium.

The Plenary Council will shape the direction of the Church in Australia for decades to come.

Seeing with spiritual eyes

It is critical that we see the current challenges facing the Church as fundamentally spiritual in nature and recognise that they are part of the spiritual battle in which every Christian is engaged.

As human beings who rely heavily on our physical senses in everyday life we can easily forget that we are also spiritual beings. Many difficulties we encounter are primarily spiritual in nature or have their source in the spiritual order. We are in a spiritual battle where there are spiritual forces, some trying to assist us while others attempt to lead us astray.

When the Lord responded to the testing question of the Pharisees and Scribes about providing a sign to authenticate his identity and mission, he said that they could readily read the signs from the weather, but they could not interpret the "signs of the times" (see Mt 16:1-3). Jesus accused them of having the ability to interpret physical phenomena but not being able to read what is happening at the spiritual level.

This was not an isolated instance for Jesus. On many occasions he challenged people to have spiritual perception in order to see what God is doing. When asked why he turned to the use of parables in his teaching, he referred to a prophesy of Isaiah: "They may indeed see but not perceive, and may indeed hear but not understand" (see Mk 4:12). At times when the Lord concluded a significant piece of teaching he said, "He who has ears to hear, let him hear" (Mt 11:15, see also Mk 4:9, 23).

We are reminded that while we may readily interpret things at the natural level, we can fail to interpret things at the supernatural level. To have spiritual insight we need to be alert and attuned to the spiritual world.

Currently, there are such radical forces at work in the culture creating disorientation and confusion that our own spiritual perception is constantly under attack; genuine spiritual discernment has become increasingly difficult.

The only way to ensure our spiritual perception and reading of the signs of the times is authentically Christian is to immerse ourselves in the rich and inspiring expression of the Catholic faith we find in Sacred Scripture, the Apostolic Tradition and the teaching contained in the Magisterium. These sources provide the basis for our spiritual perception, and having spiritual perception to properly discern what is happening is vitally important. These sources are grounded in Christ. The Christian, the person of faith who seeks the way of Christ, can only read the "signs of the times" through Christ. We cannot just view the strong currents shaping our history as only having a human or physical dimension. They have a spiritual component which can be either the work of God or the work of the Evil One. Jesus referred to Satan as the "ruler of this world" (see Jn 12:31). We must view the movements of our time as either being open to the action of God, or opposed to the transcendent good and ultimately driven by the actions of the Evil One.

It is only through a Christocentric approach that we will gain the necessary spiritual perception to properly discern the meaning of events in the world and formulate the authentically Christian response.

What is the way ahead?

A clear discernment of what is happening is necessary at the spiritual level. To see with the eyes of faith is critical in enabling us to map a way ahead. This applies to the individual Catholic and to the Catholic community as a whole. This is particularly relevant as the Church in Australia reflects on how it might best address the challenges that confront her through the Plenary Council scheduled for October 2021 and then July 2022.

This short book reflects on the future of the Church in the light of the current cultural situation in Australia. It offers a number of avenues in which Catholics, both lay and clerical, can work for a strengthening of Catholic life so that solid foundations can be laid to ensure future growth.

If we take this opportunity offered by the Plenary Council to lay solid and sound foundations for the Church we can ensure that there is a platform in place when the time for renewed flourishing of Catholic life occurs.

This work is ultimately intended to offer some possible ways we might address the current difficult situation we find ourselves in as a Church in Australia, and by doing so this book seeks to positively contribute to the discussion leading up the first session of the Plenary Council.

The spiritual inspiration for this book is the promise of the Lord that He is with His Church until the end of time (see Mt 28:20). The Lord has promised to protect His Church. He may appear to be asleep as the disciples experienced during the storm on the Sea of Galilee. They were alarmed at the threat the fierce winds and seas presented. In their panic they cried, "Teacher, do you not care if we perish?" (Mk 4:38). The Lord's response is worth noting: "Why are you afraid? Have you no faith?" (Mk 4:40).

Each of us needs to be alert to the "signs of the times", but these can only be approached through a spirit of faith. There is a great temptation to approach this discernment subjectively, imposing our own subjective feelings and emotions. However, this would be a false discernment. We cannot just view things on the human level alone. Like the disciples we need to see with the eyes of faith so that we can interpret correctly what is happening around us.

This book seeks to offer a reading of the times alert to the spiritual movements which are afoot. Having spiritual insight into our times provides us with the means to propose a way forward for ourselves as living stones making up the spiritual house which is the Church (see I Pet 2:5).

The Church in Australia can respond to the "signs of the times" with a spirit of deep faith. The Plenary Council offers us a unique opportunity to do this. Developing sound pastoral and spiritual foundations can enable the Church here in Australia to be spurred on by a confident trust that the Lord is present and at work amongst us. So, we can face the future with hope and purpose.

2

Christ – the Foundation

The Second Vatican Council in its document on the Church in the Modern World, *Gaudium et Spes*, gives clear witness to the understanding that it is only in Christ that human life can be understood and truly lived:

> The truth is that only in the mystery of the incarnate Word does the mystery of man take on light. For Adam, the first man, was a figure of Him Who was to come, namely Christ the Lord. Christ, the final Adam, by the revelation of the mystery of the Father and His love, fully reveals man to man himself and makes his supreme calling clear. It is not surprising, then, that in Him all the aforementioned truths find their root and attain their crown. (*GS* 22)

The problems we face are significant. The only way to begin to grapple with how we should respond is by first going to He who is The Way, Christ Jesus. In Christ we have the mystery of the human person fully revealed and ultimately it is only in Christ that the world and all of creation is restored.

Christ is the foundation for the Christian life. Christ is the foundation for the life and mission of the Church. At this moment in our history it is essential that our faith is grounded in Christ.

Let us firstly examine what it means to have a faith grounded in Christ.

Baptismal conversion

At the heart of such a faith is our baptismal conversion. The Apostles understood clearly the process by which a person was to become a Christian. Following his bold preaching to the crowds on Pentecost morning St Peter was asked by those convicted by his preaching, who were "cut to the heart", as St Luke records, "what must we do brothers?" St Peter did not hesitate: "Repent and be baptised every one of you in the name of Jesus Christ for the forgiveness of your sins; and you shall receive the gift of the Holy Spirit" (Acts 2:38). At His Ascension Jesus had given them clear instruction: "Go therefore and make disciples of all the nations, baptising them in the name of the Father, and of the Son and of the Holy Spirit" (Mt 28:19). Baptism is the entry point into the Christian life and establishes a pattern of daily conversion to the Lord.

There are two requirements made of the person who is to receive Baptism. They are expressed clearly in the Baptismal Promises which are made at the celebration of the sacrament and renewed solemnly at Easter each year. There is a renunciation of Satan and a profession of faith in the Triune God – Father, Son and Holy Spirit.

In the baptismal ceremony the priest asks the question: Do you renounce Satan? And all his works? And all his empty show? To which we reply: I do.

Based on this threefold rejection of evil, the priest continues and asks us whether we embrace the Apostolic faith: Do you believe in God, the Father Almighty, Creator of heaven and earth? Do you believe in Jesus Christ, his only Son, our Lord, Who was born of the Virgin Mary, suffered death and was buried, rose again from the dead and is seated at the right hand of the Father? Do you believe in the Holy Spirit, the holy Catholic Church, the communion of saints, the forgiveness of sins, the resurrection of the body, and life everlasting? To which we reply: I do.

This liturgical formula gives expression to what the Lord required of those who wanted to respond to his preaching as he commenced his public ministry: "The time is fulfilled, and the kingdom of God is at hand; repent and believe" (Mk 1:14). The two expressions of response are repentance and faith.

In the Rite of Christian Initiation of Adults it is recommended that the candidates receive prayers prior to Baptism. They are reminded that they reject all manner of life which is contrary to life in Christ. One example is:

> Dear candidates, the true God has called you and led you here. You sincerely desire to worship and serve him alone, and his Son Jesus Christ. Now, in the presence of this community, you must reject all rites and forms of worship that do not honour the true God. Are you determined never to abandon him and his Son Jesus Christ, and never return to the service of other masters? (RCIA 72)

This shows that the Church takes seriously the need for each candidate for baptism to reject all other spiritual influences under which they may have been prior to coming to faith in Jesus Christ. Christ alone is to be their Saviour and Lord. This reminds the believer that the Christian should avoid all spiritual influences that could pollute the pure waters of faith.

In recent decades New Age spiritualities have infiltrated parts of the Church. While individual Catholics have become involved in various New Age spiritualities like astrology, or Enneagram, or Reiki healing, New Age spiritualities have influenced some retreat and spirituality centres.

The Church has warned about the dangers of dabbling in spiritual movements which do not have a Christian origin. In 2003, a document examining the New Age was produced, entitled "Jesus Christ, The Bearer of the Water of Life". It provided a useful analysis of New Age spiritualities showing that these spiritualities are incompatible with the Catholic spiritual tradition.

In a world which is now rife with all sorts of spiritualities, the Christian should ensure that they keep away from foreign spiritual influences, drinking of the pure water provided through the Catholic spiritual tradition.

Personal encounter with Christ

A further critical part of having a faith grounded in Christ is having a personal relationship with Christ. Pope Benedict spoke often of the need for a person to have an 'encounter with Christ' to enable them to embrace the Christian life. In his first encyclical, *Deus Caritas Est*, God is love (2005), Pope Benedict presents at the very outset his understanding of the nature of Christian faith: "Being Christian is not the result of an ethical choice or a lofty idea, but the encounter with an event, a person, which gives life a new horizon and a decisive direction" (*DCE* 1). Pope Benedict knew that this encounter would be completely life-changing.

When speaking about St Paul and his conversion Pope Benedict commented to pilgrims that Paul's encounter on the road to Damascus was not with concepts or ideas but "with the person of Jesus himself." Paul "met not only the historical Jesus of the past, but the living Christ who revealed himself as the one Saviour and Lord." The encounter on the road to Damascus, he said, "caused Paul's own being to die and another to be born with the living Christ". This historical event was, he said, "true renewal, which changed all his parameters" (General Audience, 3 September 2008).

Pope Benedict went on to comment, "this transformation of his life was not the result of a psychological process, of an intellectual or moral evolution ... but the fruit of his meeting with Christ Jesus. ... St. Paul's renewal cannot be explained in any other way. Psychological analyses cannot clarify and resolve the problem; only an event, the forceful encounter with Christ, is the key to understanding what happened".

This bears some reflection. The Pope understands that coming to faith is not a psychological process. It is more than an intellectual awakening or a moral conversion. It is grounded in a personal encounter, a meeting, which occurs at the level of the heart. He adds later that this encounter is a moment when we "touch Christ's heart and feel that Christ touches ours". And concludes, "it is only in this personal relationship with Christ, in this meeting with the Risen One, that we are truly Christian".

This has significant implications for the ministry of the Church. Pope Benedict is convinced that we cannot just present an intellectual argument for Christianity to win converts to the faith. We cannot hold up some high moral ideals which may inspire someone to become Christian. Nor can we expect that faith will continue to be handed on in the family, with the support of the parish and Catholic school. This can no longer ensure that a young person will embrace the faith and choose to live it out. A person these days will believe and live out the faith by way of personal conviction more than family heritage or cultural background. Faith is no longer transmitted in some process of osmosis, but must be by intention, born of a personal decision. It is the task of the Church to facilitate such a meeting, an encounter, with the risen Christ.

The Gospels recount several stories of personal encounters with Christ. For example, the encounter of Nathaniel recorded by St

John (Jn 1:43-51). Philip had encountered Christ and came to believe in him. He sought out his friend, Nathaniel: "We have found him of whom Moses in the law and also the prophets wrote, Jesus of Nazareth, the son of Joseph". Nathaniel is sceptical and so Philip simply says, "Come and see". Philip invites Nathaniel to meet Jesus. The result is an intriguing conversation between Jesus and Nathaniel that results in him coming to believe.

In a similar way, we could examine the encounter between Jesus and the Samaritan woman at the well, told at some length by St John (Jn 4:7-30). Coming to faith in Jesus she rushes off to the village, "Come, see the man who told me everything I ever did. Can this be the Christ?"

Another example of such an encounter and a radical conversion is the story of the tax collector, Zacchaeus, who, curious about Jesus, receives the surprising request, "Zacchaeus, make haste and come down; for I must stay at your house today" (see Lk 19:1-10). By the end of the meal the tax collector embraces a complete change of heart: "Behold, Lord, the half of my goods I give to the poor; and if I have defrauded anyone of anything, I restore it fourfold". Jesus makes the simple comment upon hearing this which reveals his intent: "Today salvation has come to this house", adding, "for the Son of Man came to seek and to save what was lost".

This last comment reminds us that the singular focus of Christ in all his encounters with people was their personal salvation. He came to 'save souls'.

One man's experience of this intent of the Lord to effect conversion of life was the poet, Francis Thompson. Though a man of faith, his life was tortured and subject to addiction. Yet, he knew that God had not given up on him. In his poem, "The Hound of

Heaven", he describes his efforts to avoid God, yet he senses being constantly pursued, "I fled Him, down the nights and down the days; I fled Him, down the arches of the years; I fled Him, down the labyrinthine ways of my own mind; and in the mist of tears I hid from him".

Eventually he could not escape. God claimed him, heart and soul.

Understanding faith as principally an encounter radically alters the way in which the mission of the Church is envisaged. The task of the Church is to facilitate moments of encounter between individuals and Christ. This encounter will occur especially when both the individual Christian and the Christian community are living a life in Christ, giving clear witness to life in Christ.

Life of grace

When we consider the idea that faith is a result of an encounter with Christ and that it is Christ who is the active agent in this process, we come to an understanding that coming to faith is not a result of our own efforts or capacity to believe. We, as Christians, do not have more insight or are of nobler character than others who do not have faith.

St Paul, for example, was very conscious that he, who once persecuted the followers of Christ, was now a believer because of God's graciousness to him. It was this realisation that led him to the awareness that each person is saved by the grace and mercy of God, and not by their own efforts or good works. This is a steady theme in his writings.

In the Letter to the Ephesians this awareness is expressed in these words, "For by grace you have been saved through faith; and this is not your own doing, it is the gift of God" (Eph 2:8). He then adds, "not because of works lest any man boast".

The Christian life is always a life of grace. It is a life lived in the Holy Spirit. It is a spiritual life animated by the hidden yet transforming power of the Holy Spirit. St Paul reminds the Romans that they do not live "according to the flesh", but by the Spirit (see Rom 8:1-17).

Living an intentional Christian life

For St Paul "to live is Christ" (Phil 1:21). When he looks back on his life prior to meeting Christ, he says, "I count everything as loss because of the surpassing worth of knowing Christ Jesus my Lord" (Phil 3:8). This is how the Christian sees their identity. Christ is at the centre; He is the very heart of our life; He is the daily inspiration of our existence.

In the face of a world which is abandoning God it has become essential for spiritual survival and ultimately to ensure our eternal life that we live an intentional Christian life.

There are several critical elements to this faithful Christian existence. A summary of key elements has been provided to us by Pope St John Paul II as he outlined his spiritual strategy for the Church on the eve of the new millennium in his encyclical, *Novo Millennio Ineunte* (2001). He lists the following.

Called to holiness

The Lord sets a very clear and high standard for his followers: "You therefore must be perfect, as your heavenly Father is perfect" (Mt 5:48). As the Church approached the new millennium, Pope St John Paul II identified the call to holiness as the first and most important call for all Catholics. He said, "It is necessary therefore to rediscover the full practical significance of Chapter 5 of the Dogmatic Constitution on the Church, *Lumen Gentium*, dedicated to the "universal call to holiness". The Council Fathers laid such stress on this point, not just to embellish ecclesiology with a kind of spiritual veneer, but to make the call to holiness an intrinsic and essential aspect of their teaching on the Church (*NMI* 30).

The Pope mentions a little later that any growth in holiness depends on "the primacy of grace", warning of the futility of doing things in our own strength alone.

Prayer

The Pope then emphasises that growth in holiness can only be accomplished by a serious commitment to personal prayer. He encourages Catholics to ground themselves in the spiritual tradition of the Church: "The great mystical tradition of the Church of both East and West has much to say in this regard. It shows how prayer can progress, as a genuine dialogue of love, to the point of rendering the person wholly possessed by the divine Beloved, vibrating at the Spirit's touch, resting filially within the Father's heart" (*NMI* 33).

Amid a world which is noisy and where there is the constant chatter of voices and opinions, the Christian needs to find a quiet haven, a place where mind and heart can be stilled and focused on the presence of God. Genuine spiritual life will not be possible without a commitment to a daily time of prayer.

One form of prayer in evidence currently is Adoration of the Blessed Sacrament. Many people, especially young people, are drawn to silent adoration. There they can commune with the risen Lord who is truly present. We are also witnessing in the Church at this time a renewed love for the recitation of the Rosary, along with a deepening of devotion to the Mother of God.

Sunday Eucharist

Referring to the teaching of the Vatican Council that the celebration of the Holy Eucharist is the "source and summit of the Christian life" (*Lumen Gentium* 11; see *Catechism of the Catholic Church*, 1324), the Pope speaks of the vital role the Eucharist plays in living a life in Christ. He says, "I therefore wish to insist that sharing in the Eucharist should really be *the heart of Sunday* for every baptised person. It is a fundamental duty, to be fulfilled not just in order to observe a precept but as something felt as essential to a truly informed and consistent Christian life" (*NMI* 36).

The Pope reminds us here that Sunday Mass should not just be an hour fitted into a busy day of activity, but should be the central focus of the Lord's Day. Time with the parish community is also important to ensure that we are encouraged by the witness and example of fellow Christians.

The Mass is an act of worship of Almighty God. Among many today in the Church there is a desire for increased reverence in the way in which the Mass is celebrated. The reception of Holy Communion at Mass is an intensely personal and sacred moment in which we encounter the risen Lord.

The practice of daily Mass is something that a Catholic committed to intentional Christian life can also seek to cultivate.

Sacrament of Reconciliation

Pope John Paul knew that there is a crisis in the Church due to a loss of a sense of sin and he urges all Catholics to rediscover the efficacy of the Sacrament of Reconciliation: "My invitation then was to make every effort to face the crisis of "the sense of sin" apparent in today's culture" (*NMI* 37).

Regular use of this Sacrament is not only salutary for receiving the forgiveness of our sins, but is also an opportunity for the grace necessary to assist us in facing the temptations of life and addressing our personal points of interior struggle with sin. Regular confession helps deepen and strengthen our conscience, prone as it is to dismiss the seriousness of sin and make excuses for our failures.

Listening to the Word

Pope John Paul II encouraged the practice of reading of Sacred Scripture. He says, "There is no doubt that this primacy of holiness and prayer is inconceivable without a renewed listening to the word of God" (*NMI* 39). With our minds being bombarded with ideas and attitudes from the world around, we need to form our minds in divine truth and wisdom. Constant exposure to the Word of God will ensure that we think as God thinks and see as God sees: "For my thoughts are not your thoughts, neither are your ways my ways" (Is 55:8).

The Christian family and the parish community

To the Pope's list I would add that intentional Christian life needs to be realised within the family. Catholic parents need to ensure that their home is a place where the faith is tangibly felt and lived. Similarly, we cannot neglect the need to be an active participant in the life and mission of the parish community. The parish must be more than a 'service centre' catering for our own spiritual and pastoral needs. An intentional Catholic will seek to contribute actively to the life and mission of the parish.

Both themes will be explored in more detail in later chapters.

A missionary disciple

Pope Francis, in his first Apostolic Exhortation, *Evangelii Gaudium*, The Joy of the Gospel (2013), introduced the description of a Catholic as a "missionary disciple". This is a very useful way of describing the nature of being a Catholic.

The Pope says that "in virtue of their baptism, all members of the People of God have become missionary disciples" (*EG* 120). This means that the title is not reserved to a few. It is a call on all the baptised. He says that it would be "insufficient to envisage a plan of evangelisation to be carried out by professionals while the rest of the faithful would simply be passive recipients" (ibid). He adds, "Every Christian is a missionary to the extent that he or she has encountered the love of God in Christ Jesus: we no longer say that we are 'disciples' and 'missionaries', but rather that we are always 'missionary disciples'" (ibid).

Being a missionary disciple, he says, does not require extensive training and preparation. It is the fruit of an encounter with Christ that inspires the desire to share what we have experienced. He expects every person of faith to become an evangelist: "Every Christian is challenged, here and now, to be actively engaged in evangelisation" (ibid).

For the intentional Catholic there are everyday opportunities to share the faith with those around us. The Pope explains:

> Today, as the Church seeks to experience a profound missionary renewal, there is a kind of preaching which falls to each of us as a daily responsibility. It has to do with bringing the Gospel to the people we meet, whether they be our neighbours or complete strangers. This is the informal preaching which takes place in the middle of a conversation, something along the lines of what a missionary does when visiting a home. Being a disciple means being constantly ready to bring the love of Jesus to others, and this can happen unexpectedly and in any place: on the street, in a city square, during work, on a journey (*EG* 127).

Pope Francis has presented a fresh way of seeing our identity as Catholics. In facing the evident challenges of the rapidly changing circumstances in which we now live, this identity must not only be acknowledged but embraced. It is important also that we do not attempt this alone. We need others with us and around us, a "cloud of witnesses" (Heb 12:1) to spur us on.

Grounded in a personal response to Christ

As the Church in Australia prepares for the Plenary Council, all discernment about the future of the life and mission of the Church needs to be firmly grounded in a personal response to Christ. The Church cannot but proclaim the call to conversion and faith as the foundation for all that is proposed.

The way of Christ is the path to live a life that is authentically Christian. This is how the Catholic community can become the missionary disciples so needed in our society today.

3

The Cultural Shift

We are witnessing significant changes in our Australian culture. We must acknowledge that we have arrived at the current cultural situation, not purely be chance or coincidence, but as a result of very determined and powerful social movements which have sought to throw off the Christian values which once guided our Australian society.

There are forces seeking to overturn the influence of Christianity and they have made very significant advances in recent decades. Our social and civic structures are being reshaped by dominant cultural movements that are antagonistic to the Christian faith. This will have far reaching influence on the quality of life within our society. It will also have effect on the life and mission of the Church.

Changes in legislation

Over recent decades there has been a steady march of legislative change on issues that go the heart of what it is to be a human person and the value and meaning of human life. From the legislation on abortion and euthanasia to the legislative redefinition of marriage, sex and gender. In effect these amount to a determined effort to remove the Christian moral underpinning to our society. Despite efforts by Christians to resist these changes, they have swept across the various state and federal jurisdictions in Australia and across the Western world. And the pace and radicalness of change is increasing. Accompanying these legislative changes have been efforts both legal and cultural to silence the voice of Christians from even stating the most basic teachings of their faith in public.

The two principal theatres of social change have been in the areas of the sacredness of human life and the nature and purpose of human sexuality. Additionally, limitations on religious freedom mean that the ability of a Christian to speak publicly in opposition to such changes is jeopardised. In the near future a Christian may be judged a criminal for so doing.

On human life

Changes to laws concerning abortion began to occur in the late 1960s. The landmark Supreme Court ruling in Victoria in 1969 ('the Menhennitt ruling') established that an abortion will be lawful if a person had an honest belief on reasonable grounds that the abortion was both 'necessary' and 'proportionate.' Other states soon followed. Over time further relaxation of circumstances in which an abortion could be sought spread across the jurisdictions. Abortion has now become quite commonplace and many people in Australia view it as a right.

Legislation was introduced in Tasmania in 2013 that expanded access to abortion and sought to prevent any form of protest outside an abortion clinic by the application of an exclusion zone. Expressions of opposition, even when peaceful and prayerful, were denied. The Legislation requires doctors to co-operate with referral for abortion, even if they conscientiously object. Threats to freedom of conscience are now very real.

With the passing of the *Voluntary Assisted Dying Act 2017* in Victoria, and in Tasmania in 2021, the state now approves medically assisting a person to commit suicide. Each new piece of legislation further relaxes the safeguards, and so the 'culture of death' grows.

On marriage

The 2017 public plebiscite in Australia on changing the legal definition of marriage to include same sex couples was a watershed moment in Australian culture. We had previously prided ourselves as being a nation of the 'fair go' and were generally respectful towards those having different views from ourselves. We believed that everyone had a right to express their opinion, and we encouraged open debate. However, the process leading up to the postal vote revealed something quite different.

Those advocating the "No" position found themselves subject to nasty vilification and abuse. They were readily called 'homophobe' or 'bigot'. They were subject to threats and intimidation. Venues that were booked for meetings of the "No" campaign received threats and many out of fear of retribution chose not to offer their services to the "No" campaign. Some 1,300 corporations were signed up to support the "Yes" campaign, and a number of individuals or business who didn't where threatened with loss of custom.

The vehement opposition to the Christian understanding of marriage and to those who sought to articulate it during this debate revealed not only the rise of a militant rejection of Christianity, but an intent to supress the Christian voice in society. This was not just a cultural struggle but a high stakes spiritual battle.

On sex and gender dysphoria

The emerging social phenomena of young people wanting to be identified and treated as if they are of the opposite sex has led to legislative changes in Tasmanian law whereby a person can change their birth certificate to reflect how they view their gender identity.

More recently a number of states had passed legislation in relation to so-called sexual orientation and gender conversion therapy, including Queensland, the ACT and Victoria, making it illegal to try to counsel someone against seeking medical or legal intervention to change their appearance and legal gender classification.

The transgender movement cuts to the heart of the meaning of the human person. Pope Benedict argued that "man too has a nature that he must respect and that he cannot manipulate at will" (Address, Berlin, 22 September 2011). Pope Francis has raised his voice saying that people cannot choose their genders. Speaking to a group of Polish bishops in 2016, Pope Francis criticised teaching children that they can choose their gender identity. He said, "Today, children are taught this at school: that everyone can choose their own sex." He added, "God created man and woman; God created the world like this and we are doing the exact opposite."

In 2019, the Congregation for Catholic Education produced a text, *Male and Female He Created Them*, to help Catholic teachers, parents, students and clergy address what it called an "educational crisis" in the field of sex education.

On threats to religious freedom

Alongside these ideological legislative changes, which now allow people to pursue their individual choices concerning their sexuality and life matters, laws are also introduced to prohibit resistance to these changes.

In Australia, it is unlawful to discriminate on the basis of a number of protected attributes including age, disability, race, sex, intersex status, gender identity and sexual orientation. Various anti-discrimination laws have been passed at both federal and state levels.

Since 1998, the *Anti-Discrimination Act* in Tasmania has prohibited behaviour which is felt to cause "offence" to another person on the basis of a particular characteristic. It has meant that the Commissioner has the power to investigate anyone who is deemed to have caused offence to someone on the basis of one of the protected attributes. If the matter is taken further and brought before the Anti-Discrimination Tribunal, after their inquiry the Tribunal can make an "order" which can include prohibiting the public expression of what was found to be offensive, redress to the complainant, of the imposition of a fine. Thus, in my own situation, if the complaint against me had continued to the Tribunal stage and been upheld, I could have had an order issued against me preventing me from publicly teaching the Catholic belief that marriage is between a man and a woman. This would be on the basis that someone has found themselves "offended" by the expression of this teaching. Such legislation has a "chilling effect" on freedom of speech whereby people do not dare to express their deeply felt beliefs on matters like the nature of marriage for fear of being hauled up before the Anti-Discrimination Commissioner. This is not only the case in formal situations, but we are now at a point where even casual conversation can become the subject of review by the Anti-Discrimination Commissioner and Tribunal.

Anti-discrimination legislation could also be used to investigate parents who voice legitimate concerns about their child wanting to change their so-called gender identity. The state can intervene if it is determined that parents have in some way discriminated or engaged in any conduct which offends, humiliates, intimidates, insults or ridicules their child by opposing their child's efforts to change their gender. Such behaviour by parents could be regarded as infringing the legislation.

On the powerful influence of social media

Much of this type of legislation is increasingly motivated by the development of identity politics. Minority groups are vocal in demanding their rights. In more recent times the 'cancel culture' trend has further weaponised individual and minority group ideologies.

Legislation, which has as the intention of providing a shield for the vulnerable, has been made into a weapon against those who do not subscribe to the prevailing cultural trends.

In this new social environment of insistence on personal rights we have witnessed the rise of vicious social media attacks that are levelled against people under the veil of anonymity. These can be extraordinarily damaging, sometimes emotionally crippling individuals and on occasions leading people to take their lives.

The social media world has become a brutal environment. It has become a place of mob rule where individuals are mercilessly targeted. We can see in all of this the serious decline in public decency as well as serious threats to freedom of speech. Society, and indeed democracy, are the poorer for these disturbing trends.

A culture of death

Pope St John Paul II, the great champion of the sacredness of human life, spoke of this powerful movement in the culture to overturn the Christian understanding of human life describing it as "the culture of death". In his encyclical, *Evangelium Vitae*, The Gospel of Life, (1995) he said,

This situation, with its lights and shadows, ought to make us all fully aware that we are facing an enormous and dramatic clash between good and evil, death and life, the "culture of death" and the "culture of life". We find ourselves not only "faced with" but necessarily "in the midst of" this conflict: we are all involved and we all share in it, with the inescapable responsibility of choosing to be unconditionally pro-life" (*EV* 28).

He is under no illusion that there is "an enormous and dramatic clash between good and evil". He identifies a rising "culture of death" coming upon humanity which he does not deny has an evil dimension. There are, to his mind, "principalities and powers" at work.

Rejection of truth and the dictatorship of relativism

At the beginning of the 2005 conclave to elect a new pope, Cardinal Ratzinger preached a now-famous homily condemning what he called the "dictatorship of relativism", further building on the insights of Pope Saint John Paul II. He warned: "We are building a dictatorship of relativism that does not recognise anything as definitive and whose ultimate goal consists solely of one's own ego and desires". These are strong words which elicited much comment at the time.

Cardinal Ratzinger expressed his concern, not only about what is happening in the broader culture, but he was concerned about the effects it was having upon ordinary members of the Church. He said that if Catholics were not mature in faith they would be swept along by the current of popular ideas. He observed:

> The thought of many Christians has often been tossed about by these waves, tossed from one end to the other: from Marxism to liberalism, to libertinism, from collectivism to radical individualism, from atheism to religious mysticism, from agnosticism to syncretism.

The issue for the average Catholic is whether their faith is strong enough to resist the tide of social change. Sadly, now in the Church, there are many who think more with the world in all its secularity than with the tradition of the faith.

Natural law and the Christian view of the human person

As an antidote to the rise of relativism and its influence on legislation, the Church teaches that there are immutable moral absolutes. God the Creator invested not only the physical universe with laws to ensure its proper functioning but also the human person. It is through what Catholic theology refers to as the "natural law" that we are able to discern the God's Eternal law as it relates to human beings. It is through the natural law that we are able to discern the higher moral law which sits above and governs human civil law.

Our moral obligations and rights flow from God's moral law alone. An awareness of the existence of a natural law predates Christianity and some of the earliest references to it can be found in ancient Greek writings, in particular the philosophers, Socrates, Plato and Aristotle. However, Christian thought has elevated this significant philosophical insight. The higher, or objective moral law that they recognised, was for the Christian, none other than God's moral law. The embodiment of God's plan for humanity and how to realise human flourishing.

In his encyclical, *Veritatis Splendor,* The Splendour of Truth (1993), Pope St John Paul II asserts that there are absolute truths which are accessible to human reason. Contrary to the philosophy of moral relativism, the encyclical says that natural moral law is universal across all peoples in varying cultures, and is in fact rooted in the human condition. The Pope teaches that no matter how separated someone is from God, "in the depths of his heart there always remains a yearning for absolute truth and a thirst to attain full knowledge of it" (*VS* 1).

The encyclical adds that the capacity of the human person to recognise moral truths is complemented and completed by divine revelation expressed in Sacred Scripture.

Christianity possesses a wonderful vision of the human person, inspired by the revelation of Sacred Scripture that we are created in the image and likeness of God. The Christian understands the reality of sin but knows the salvation won for us by Christ is always at hand. The Christian lives with an abiding hope because they know the reality of God's love and mercy. However, this understanding is fast becoming lost as the world not only denies God but even the existence of objective truth.

We need to again speak out against the denial of objective moral truth and proclaim that there is an objective moral truth that cannot be avoided.

Loss of the Christian vision of society

Since the time that the Emperor Constantine ended government persecution of Christians, Christianity has played a central role guiding Western civilisation. Christianity promotes the notion of the dignity of the human person and the sanctity of marriage and family life. It has fostered care for the poor and suffering. Christianity has encouraged the pursuit of justice. It has freed women from servitude in many cultures. It has advanced the rule of law whereby a person is innocent until proven guilty. Western society is in debt to Christianity in the way that it has fashioned its democratic spirit and the value of individual freedom.

Christianity has not only been of benefit to individuals in seeking a path of virtue but has shaped many of the elements in our society which have promoted the wellbeing of its citizens. Over the centuries Christianity has shaped Western civilisation and endowed it with qualities that ennoble human life.

While it is true that a majority of Australians profess to be Christian and many hold to a view of life shaped by a Christian understanding, there are powerful forces in our society that repudiate the significant contribution Christianity has made and continues to make to the good of human society. They are determined to develop a new social order without reference to God or to our Christian heritage.

The Christian vision of life which has shaped our society is not being passed on in any comprehensive and systematic way, as happened in the past, and there is now a generation who lack knowledge of the fundamental beliefs of the Christian faith, nor appreciate the contribution it has made and continues to make to our social fabric. They are easily affected by various social media 'influencers' who present a way of living which is devoid of Christian virtue. Their thinking is easily shaped by the many ideologically loaded courses at university or by media-fanned ideas which promote the radical individualism of identity politics.

Our society is adopting a path that has abandoned not only faith in God but also belief in the true nature and dignity of the human person. Ultimately it is only belief in God that can protect this dignity.

One result of this is that, in the face of new legislation on social/moral issues, politicians who retain a commitment to Christian moral and spiritual principles now find themselves in the minority in the parliament. They are unable to stop the flow of legislation which they know is ultimately destructive of family and society. Many parliamentarians who genuinely seek what is good find themselves pressured to accept popular opinion and are forced to compromise with the demands of aggressive vocal minorities who advocate defective social change.

History has taught us that without sound spiritual and moral foundations a society will ultimately flounder; and the cost in human terms will be great. We are already witnessing a dramatic rise in many social ills like the increase in family breakdown, the increased incidence of drug taking and the rise in abuse and suicide, yet we fail to attribute these to abandoning the truth of Christian moral teaching.

Sadly, many Christians have been persuaded that they need to be "on the right side of history" and urge the Church to get with the times and change its moral teaching. There is an increasing number of voices within the Church who are publicly promoting views contrary to Catholic teaching on matters like sexuality, marriage, and life. They have lost sight of the Christian understanding of the human person and instead adopted the dominant understanding of person in the culture where affirmation of one's self identity is the highest or most important value.

Many who are baptised and have only some cultural allegiance to the Church are more shaped in their minds by the secular world around than by the teaching of the Church. They readily become critical of the Church which they regard as backward and irrelevant. They are no longer able to see with the eyes of faith. They have allowed themselves to be conformed to the thinking of the world.

This phenomenon is the result of a failure of the Church in many places to provide sound catechesis to the young. We as a Church have not ensured the effective transmission of the faith. This will be explored more in the following chapters.

Pope St John Paul II saw the intrinsic link between a loss of a sense of God and the outworking of this on our understanding of the human person. He explained:

> In seeking the deepest roots of the struggle between the "culture of life" and the "culture of death", we cannot restrict ourselves to the perverse idea of freedom mentioned above. We have to go to the heart of the tragedy being experienced by modern man: the eclipse of the sense of God and of man, typical of a social and cultural climate dominated by secularism, which, with its ubiquitous tentacles, succeeds at times in putting Christian communities themselves to the test. Those who allow themselves to be influenced by this climate easily fall into a sad vicious circle: when the sense of God is lost, there is also a tendency to lose the sense of man, of his dignity and his life; in turn, the systematic violation of the moral law, especially in the serious matter of respect for human life and its dignity, produces a kind of progressive darkening of the capacity to discern God's living and saving presence. (EV 21)

We are witnessing in our society, at an increasing rate, the rejection of the teachings of the Christian faith, both directly and indirectly. There have been for some time powerful cultural movements seeking to eliminate the Christian influence in the culture. With the significant rise of those who claim to have no commitment to a particular community of faith, our society is being reshaped by anti-Christian forces. The significance of this cannot be underestimated. Our culture is sailing into unchartered waters, namely a new era of self worship, where the individual self is understood as the highest authority. What is particularly significant about this change is that the loss of Christian faith in our society does not involve a return some kind of pre-Christian paganism, which at least recognised some higher transcendent power or authority. Rather, it involves a rejection of any kind of transcendent authority and replaces this with the self.

What is clearly now in evidence in our culture is the pervasiveness of a view about the nature of human life that fails to acknowledge God as its origin and destiny. This has now corrupted the understanding even of many in the Church. The world has 'evangelised' the Church, rather than the Church evangelising the world.

Every culture, if it is to be lasting and enriching of human life, needs to have a positive spiritual underpinning. Western civilisation has been formed and directed by Christianity, which has provided its spiritual foundation. These spiritual roots have also provided the moral beliefs that guided Western civilisation. When addressing the United Nations in 1965, Pope St Paul VI said, "To put it in a word, the edifice of modern civilisation has to be built on spiritual principles, for they are the only ones capable not only of supporting it, but of shedding light on it and inspiring it. And we are convinced, as you know, that these indispensable principles of higher wisdom cannot rest on anything but faith in God" (Address to United Nations, 1965, 4).

There is a very disturbing comment by the Lord which warns of the possible condition of the world upon his return: "When the Son of Man comes, will he find faith on earth?" (Lk 18:8). Indeed, when the Lord speaks about his final coming he describes a world not ready and receptive, but a world that is lost and heaving under all sorts of distress. In Matthew 24 the Lord gives warnings of much tribulation that must come upon the world prior to his return in glory.

To evangelise the culture

It will only be through prayer and evangelisation that this situation will be turned around. One of the most important roles of the Church is the evangelisation of culture. As the Catholic Church in Australia meets to discern its future course, a central focus must be the evangelisation of culture. A key to effective evangelisation will of course be the work and life of Catholic lay people who live in the midst of society and have a sense of mission. To achieve this lay Catholics will need to be formed more fully in the Christian vision of life and spiritually equipped to engage in the struggle for the future direction of our society.

The formation of a generation of Catholic men and women to be "salt and light" in all levels of Australian society is one of the vital challenges that should be addressed in the deliberations of the Plenary Council.

The Christian vision of human life is good, not only for the individual as a path for salvation, but it is the leaven that can transform society in a way that all can flourish. Christian men and women, alive in faith and well formed in the Christian life, can transform the culture. We have the truth which we know the human heart desires. As Chesterton famously said, "It is not that the Catholic faith has been tried and found wanting, it simply has not been tried", at least not the authentic understanding of the Catholic faith. The task before us is immense, but all things as possible with God.

4

Rebuilding a Culture of Marriage and Family

Up until the 1960s, Australian society was guided, at least in a very basic way, by the Christian moral ideal for human sexuality, marriage and family.

Male and female were viewed as sexually complementary and sexual relationships were viewed as only appropriate between a married man and woman. Marriage was viewed as a life-long relationship which had both a romantic and procreative purpose; it was for love, but also for having children and raising a family. The sex of a person was confirmed at birth through biology and if there was some dysphoria between one's perception of the self and one's body this was considered to be a pathology to be treated.

The primary role of the husband or father was to provide for his family through paid work and the primary role of the woman or mother was to work in the home caring for the children and ensuring the proper running of the household.

Despite the fact that many were not able to live up to this ideal, what was important was that it remained the ideal. At least publicly it remained the guiding standard of public morality. What has changed in the last fifty years, and is unprecedented in human history, is the successful challenge to this ideal on a civilisational level. While groups and movements throughout history had sought to challenge this Christian ideal in particular countries, they had been unsuccessful. It was only from the 1960s onwards that these efforts started to make real inroads, resulting in recent years the effective rejection of this Christian ideal of human sexuality, marriage and family.

There is now no single consistent guiding vision as such for Australian society, rather there is simply the principle of individual choice as the guiding ideal, which it is believed should only be limited if such exercise of the choice would harm others in some way. The guiding moral principle for Western civilisation would seem to be "individuals should be free to be and do whatever they want as long as it does not involve harming others".

More recently the notion of harming others has been extended to not just physical harm, or speech that promotes physical harm or violence, but emotional harm or anything that causes offence.

How far we have come! We are reaping the whirlwind generated by the 'Sexual Revolution' and there is further our culture will go.

The face of marriage and family is being reshaped by powerful cultural forces in movies, books, television series, advertising and social media. They have and continue to exert a major influence in changing people's values and lifestyles.

Marriage and family life have been severely impacted. Marriages break down leaving the couple damaged and disillusioned and the children wounded and confused. Couples, in choosing to cohabit, weaken their ability to embrace the discipline of stable commitment. The increase in domestic violence reflects new levels of pain and suffering in relationships. The deaths of so many children in the womb by means of abortion leave enduring pain and deep scars on those involved. There is much confusion among young people about how to enter healthy and life-giving relationships. Their understanding of the nature of sexuality has been corrupted by the distorted understanding of human sexuality presented in popular culture and especially by the easy access to pornography. Turning to drugs reflects insecurity and alienation.

It is the case now that people are largely shaped in their thinking by the new cultural patterns, even if some lament the loss of conventional morality. Young people have largely abandoned the Christian approach to sexuality and marriage. The numbers of young Catholics seeking a sacramental marriage have plummeted in recent decades.

It is possible to list issue after issue that has altered the way in which marriage and family is now understood and lived within our society. We are facing a deep crisis that cries out for resolution. In a world that has been shaped by the sexual revolution, Christianity offers an alternative vision for sexuality, marriage and family. The Christian understanding captures God's good plan to ensure the flourishing of human life. It has become necessary to rebuild a culture of Christian marriage and family in the hope that the society will come to see that there is an answer to all the suffering and anguish that now characterises human relationships.

A prophesy

Cardinal Caffarra, former Archbishop of Bologna, who died in 2017, was a tireless defender of Catholic doctrine on marriage and the family. In 1981 he was asked by Pope St John Paul II to found a Pontifical Institute for Studies on Marriage and Family. From the beginning of his long pontificate Pope St John Paul II had sought to promote Catholic teaching on marriage and family. From September 1979 the Pope delivered a systematic catechesis on this subject which was intended as a deeper explanation of the teaching of Pope St Paul VI in his encyclical on human life, *Humanae Vitae* (1968). This teaching has become popularly known as "Theology of the Body". The founding of the Institute met with some resistance within certain quarters of the Church. Cardinal Caffarra wrote to Sr Maria Lucia of Jesus, one of the visionaries of Fatima, to request her prayers. In reply the Carmelite nun sent a message that the Cardinal revealed only in recent times. He said:

> In [her letter] we find written: "The final battle between the Lord and the reign of Satan will be about marriage and the family. Don't be afraid," she added, "because anyone who operates for the sanctity of marriage and the family will always be contended and opposed in every way, because this is the decisive issue." And then she concluded: "However, Our Lady has already crushed its head."

These are very significant words. We know that we now face a critical struggle for God's plan for marriage and family. While the task appears monumental, and it is, the visionary offered hope when she said, "Our Lady has already crushed its head".

The Creator's intention for sex and gender

In the context of the discussion about sex and gender in our society, the Church holds a vision of the human person that "sees sexuality as a fundamental component of one's personhood" (*Male and Female He Created Them*, 4). Hence while men and women as individuals both share an equal dignity before God, they are fundamentally different expressions of the human person. The sexual differences between men and women do not stem from purely biological differences but also exist at a psychological and spiritual level. This sexual difference "is not meant to stand in opposition, or to subordinate, but is for the sake of communion and generation" (Pope Francis, General Audience, 15 April 2015). This difference is ontological at the level of personhood, over and above biology, but is made visible through a sexually differentiated body. Additionally, a complementary relationship exists between men and women. God made Adam and Eve, not for solitude, but for each other. When a man and woman are united through marriage, their union creates a whole that is greater than the sum of the parts. This is all part of the wisdom of the Creator.

Recent changes in legislation and new political ideologies have emerged to challenge the Church's understanding of sex and gender. Gender ideology is based on the idea that "denies the difference and reciprocity in nature of a man and a woman and envisages a society without sexual differences" (Pope Francis, *Amoris Laetitia*, 56). On this understanding the sex and gender of a person become radically separated and their gender becomes a fluid reality. In contrast, the Church acknowledges that sex and gender can be distinguished, but not be separated.

Promoting the virtue of chastity

The Church has long promoted the virtue of chastity. In the broader secular culture, it is a forgotten and ignored virtue. The *Catechism of the Catholic Church* teaches, "Chastity means the successful integration of sexuality within the person and thus the inner unity of man in his bodily and spiritual being. Sexuality, in which man's belonging to the bodily and biological world is expressed, becomes personal and truly human when it is integrated into the relationship of one person to another, in the complete and lifelong mutual gift of a man and a woman" (*CCC* 2337).

At the heart of growing in the virtue of chastity is the discipline by which a person is able to master their passions so that they are directed to their proper purpose. The Church expresses this in the Catechism in these words, "The chaste person maintains the integrity of the powers of life and love placed in him. This integrity ensures the unity of the person; it is opposed to any behaviour that would impair it. It tolerates neither a double life nor duplicity in speech". (*CCC* 2338)

Growing in chastity as a single person lays a foundation for its place later in marriage and for those who take a formal vow of chastity as part of their ordination to the priesthood or consecration to religious life. The development of this virtue helps the growth of the human person as it promotes not just self-discipline but also helps a person to be other-directed in relationships.

There is an increasing need to publicly explain and promote the Church's beautiful and life affirming teaching about human sexuality, which includes the moral problem of sexual activity outside the covenant of marriage. This teaching is grounded in Sacred Scripture. Sexual relationships outside the covenant of marriage betray God's plan for humanity and attack the sexual integrity and flourishing of the person. They are sinful and harmful to the person. No matter how challenging it is to present this teaching, it is vital that the Church does not shy away from what it knows as the truth about the meaning and purpose of human sexuality.

In relation to the question of those who experience same-sex attraction the Church also proposes the virtue of chastity. The teaching of the Catholic Church on this matter provides a path for the human flourishing. Its teaching is given as a service to assist a person find a path for true happiness in accord with the plan of God for human sexuality. It is offered with compassion:

> The number of men and women who have deep-seated homosexual tendencies is not negligible. This inclination, which is objectively disordered, constitutes for most of them a trial. They must be accepted with respect, compassion, and sensitivity. Every sign of unjust discrimination in their regard should be avoided. These persons are called to fulfil God's will in their lives and, if they are Christians, to unite to the sacrifice of the Lord's Cross the difficulties they may encounter from their condition. (*CCC* 2358)

For any person who experiences same-sex attraction or gender dysphoria the Church teaches: "... no one should suffer bullying, violence, insults or unjust discrimination based on their specific characteristics" (*Male and Female He Created Them*, 16).

While such teaching is considered by many to be out of touch with contemporary society, it is consistent with the plan of God for human sexuality and the recipe for healthy and life-giving relationships. In promoting the virtue of chastity the Church has a message which ensures healthy human life and sound and enduring relationships.

A domestic church

The current situation is dire indeed and calls for serious effort. One key approach is to urge and enable Catholic couples to embrace "Intentional Catholic family life." At the heart of this is a decision, a commitment made by the couple, to become a strong Catholic family. Joshua declared: "as for me and my house we will serve the Lord" (Jos 24:15). This decision taken by a couple will direct and inspire actions that foster Catholic life within the family.

A Catholic couple can be helped to fashion an understanding of what intentional Catholic family life means if they view their family as the "domestic Church". This designation of the family is embedded deeply in our Catholic tradition. In *Gratissimam Sane*, his "Letter to Families" (1994) Pope St John Paul II said, "The Fathers of the Church, in the Christian tradition, have spoken of the family as a 'domestic church,' a 'little church.'" (*GS* 3). He added, "In our own times we have often returned to the phrase 'domestic church', which the Council adopted and the sense of which we hope will always remain alive in people's minds. This desire is not lessened by an awareness of the changed conditions of families in today's world" (ibid). The notion is found in the *Catechism of the Catholic Church* (*CCC* 1656) revealing that this idea has richness and significance. It is a way of understanding the family from a perspective of faith.

The Pope, in saying that the family is the "way of the Church", speaks of the evident human reality:

> It is a path common to all, yet one which is particular, unique and unrepeatable, just as every individual is unrepeatable; it is a path from which man cannot withdraw. Indeed, a person normally comes into the world within a family, and can be said to owe to the family the very fact of his existing as an individual. When he has no family, the person coming into the world develops an anguished sense of pain and loss, one which will subsequently burden his whole life (*GS* 2).

The family is the bedrock of human society and the bedrock of the Christian community. When a family embraces this vision of itself it as a "domestic church", it becomes possible to become an influence both in the Church and in the culture.

There are some simple elements to fostering this vision for family life. It begins with family prayer. Grace before meals, morning and night prayers with the children, the family Rosary, celebrating baptismal or 'name' days, have always been part of traditional Catholic family life.

In speaking about the importance of prayer in the family the Pope says:

> Prayer increases the strength and spiritual unity of the family, helping the family to partake of God's own "strength". In the solemn nuptial blessing during the Rite of Marriage, the celebrant calls upon the Lord in these words: "Pour out upon them the grace of the Holy Spirit so that by your love poured into their hearts they will remain faithful in the marriage covenant". This "visitation" of the Holy Spirit gives rise to the inner strength of families, as well as the power capable of uniting them in love and truth. (*GS* 4)

Marriage is a sacrament. As the Pope reminds us, a Catholic couple have explicitly invited God – Father, Son and Holy Spirit – to enter their relationship and subsequently their family life. A Christian couple know that God wants to be an integral part of their life. God just doesn't just look on, but is actively involved. This is how the Church understands the sacramentality of marriage.

A couple who are committed to making their marriage a domestic church will want their home to reflect this. So the home will have signs of its character. It will be evidently a Catholic home with a crucifix, a statue of the Virgin Mary, other traditional Catholic iconography in evidence to identify the home to both family members and visitors as a Christian home. An intentional Catholic family will live the liturgical seasons within the family as well as within the parish. The family will attend Mass as a family and go to confession as a family.

Essentially, the Catholic family will foster a Christian worldview in the home, helping children to assess and engage with the world in the light of the Gospel. The couple will encourage discussions on matters of faith in the hope that their children will not see faith as a private matter. The family will be the first place where children will learn to live out the Christian virtues since they will see them enacted by their parents. As witnesses to Christ, the Catholic family will be open to visitors, aware that this will be an opportunity to witness to how the Christian life can be lived.

An intentional Catholic family will forge links with other Catholic families so that their children will be aware that their family way of life is not particular to themselves.

Such efforts need to be intentional. In such ways the Catholic couple endeavour to become a little domestic church.

Engendering love

Pope St Paul VI proposed the notion that Christians are committed to the creation of what he called a "civilisation of love". In reflecting on this phrase, the Pope St John Paul, in his Letter to Families comments:

> ... the most profound meaning of the term "civilisation" is not merely political, but rather pertains to human culture. Civilisation belongs to human history because it answers man's spiritual and moral needs. Created in the image and likeness of God, man has received the world from the hands of the Creator, together with the task of shaping it in his own image and likeness. The fulfilment of this task gives rise to civilisation, which in the final analysis is nothing else than the "humanisation of the world" (*GS* 13).

Marriage and family is the place where love is engendered and purified. Love is the gift of self for the good of the other. There is no other place where this is more called forth than in marriage and family. The Pope offers this insight: "When a man and woman in marriage mutually give and receive each other in the unity of 'one flesh', the logic of the sincere gift of self becomes a part of their life. Without this, marriage would be empty; whereas a communion of persons, built on this logic, becomes a communion of parents" (*GS* 11).

The mutual gift of self in the marriage covenant moves to a new level when a child is conceived. The Pope comments, "The process from conception and growth in the mother's womb to birth makes it possible to create a space within which the new creature can be revealed as a 'gift'" (ibid).

The "hymn of love", the well-known verses of St Paul in his Letter to the Corinthians (I Cor 13:4-7), speaks of the qualities of human love that are to be engendered in marriage and family. Pope Francis in his Apostolic Exhortation, *Amoris Laetitia* (2016), on marriage and family, provides a lengthy reflection of each of the qualities listed by St Paul (see Chapter 4). As he rightly says, "For we cannot encourage a path of fidelity and mutual self-giving without encouraging the growth, strengthening and deepening of conjugal and family love" (*AL* 89).

It is in the family where a new "civilisation of love" can be born.

The dignity of the human person

The Christian has a distinctive understanding of the nature of the human person which is very different from the prevailing views in the culture.

At the heart of the Christian understanding is the Scriptural revelation found in the Book of Genesis that God created us in his "own image and likeness" (Gen 1:27). The creation account in Genesis 2 says that God breathed divine life into the human person (see Gen 2:7). Each human being has a soul.

The account of creation also speaks of God creating male and female, two equal, different and complementary ways of being human. They are intended to embrace the marital union where "the two will become one" (see Gen 2:24). Humanity was created with marriage in mind. The marriage union reflects the complementary nature of male and female.

The *Catechism of the Catholic Church* summarises the significance of this Scriptural revelation in these words:

> Being in the image of God the human individual possesses the dignity of a person, who is not just something, but someone. He is capable of self-knowledge, of self-possession and of freely giving himself and entering into communion with other persons. And he is called by grace to a covenant with his Creator, to offer him a response of faith and live that no other creature can give in his stead. (CCC 357)

These simple yet profound teachings provide the framework for Catholic teaching on the dignity of every human person, on the need to protect human life from the moment of conception to its natural end, on the nature and purpose of human sexuality and on God's good and wise plan for marriage and family.

Proclaiming Catholic teaching

Now that many jurisdictions have passed laws enshrining the destruction of human life, sexuality, marriage and family, there is an increasing challenge to ensure that the Christian understanding of the human person is not lost. This is made increasingly difficult when religious freedom is also under threat and it is more difficult to present the Christian view in the public forum.

The secular society considers many of these issues now settled and moves on to advance new causes in the construction of society devoid of Christian influence.

To ensure that those of faith do not lose sight of Christian truth we are blessed with a body of clear teaching expressed in the *Catechism of the Catholic Church* and in ordinary magisterial teaching. While there may be attempts to restrict our public profession of what we believe, it is important that we grow in deeper knowledge of the Church's teaching and find ways in which this can be passed on to the next generation.

It means finding and reading books which articulate Catholic teaching. It means seeking out sound Catholic teaching available on the internet. It means taking part in online conferences. It means discussing them in the home. In these ways we are laying solid foundations, not only for our own way of life, but helping future generations establish their lives on the rock of Catholic teaching.

Presenting this vision to the young

To rebuild a culture of marriage and family special attention needs to be given to the young. After the primary role of the family, it is through our access to the young in our extensive Catholic school system that we can offer them the Christian vision of love and life.

We have an opportunity through our Catholic schools to present, in an attractive and clear manner, the understanding of the nature of the human person. It will require a concerted effort to assist young people to see that there is another way, other than what is offered through the society around them.

It will require the work of dedicated educators who themselves are deeply imbued with the Christian vision of human life, sexuality, marriage and family, while always respecting the rights of parents. Young people can be inspired to embrace the beauty and dignity of the Christian way.

The Church's rich body of teaching on these subjects, fostered by recent popes and outlined in magisterial documents, needs to be communicated to the next generation so that they are encouraged to embrace an alternative to what they are exposed to in the society.

Families need one another

Intentional Catholic families need one another. It is difficult to lead a deeply Christian life alone. While the parish does offer much support, a family seeking to live the Christian life within the home more intensely needs to have other such families to assist them.

Families can form small groups with other Catholic families and meet together in one another's houses on a regular basis for mutual encouragement and support. In these situations parents can share their experiences and challenges. Couples can schedule a time of prayer together. They could discuss a relevant topic related to Catholic family life. Meanwhile the children enjoy time together perhaps augmented by some simple catechesis. It will be important that children become aware that their family is not the only one which is deeply faithful.

In 2017 an American social commentator, Rod Dreher, published *The Benedict Option*. It was inspired by the Benedictine communities that preserved the faith during what are commonly called the

"Dark Ages", the time of social disruption following the collapse of the Roman Empire. The book caused a good deal of discussion. Some interpreted his ideas as a complete withdrawal from society, a 'circling of the wagons'. However, his idea was more to do with finding ways to consolidate and ensure the passing on the faith during a time when society is disintegrating.

The leading moral philosopher, Alasdair MacIntyre, author of *After Virtue*, presented a similar idea:

> What matters at this stage is the construction of local forms of community within which civility and the intellectual and moral life can be sustained through the new dark ages that are already upon us. And if the tradition of the virtues was able to survive the horrors of the last dark ages, we are not entirely without grounds for hope. This time however the barbarians are not waiting behind the frontiers; they have already been governing us for quite some time. And it is our lack of consciousness of this that constitutes part of our predicament. We are waiting not for Godot, but for another – doubtless very different – St. Benedict. (*After Virtue*, p. 244)

Catholic families can find ways in which their family can live a full Christian life, supported by other similar families, and in this way their children will have a greater chance of choosing to embrace the Christian way of life.

A pastoral commitment to support marriage and family

In the face of such profound changes it may seem an impossible task to rebuild the Christian vision of sexuality, marriage and family. However, it can begin one family at a time. A renewed commitment by the Church to foster and support Christian family life can lead to the witness of happy and united families.

The Plenary Council offers an opportunity for the Church in Australia to make a decision to devote serious pastoral resources towards this critical need. The Plenary Council can be a watershed moment for a rebuilding a culture of Christian marriage and family life firstly within the Church, and then within the broader society.

5

A Renewal in Catechesis

Following from the central importance of marriage and family is the education and nurturing of the young. The Church has always sought to promote the education of the young, especially endeavouring to instil in them the Christian faith and a Christian vision for human life.

Renewal in catechesis

The Church in Australia has suffered greatly from a paucity of sound catechesis over recent decades. The time has come for a renewal in catechesis. There is a growing thirst for sound teaching, especially among the young.

The Plenary Council offers an ideal opportunity for the Church in Australia to commit to develop programs of sound catechesis. We have the blessing of the *Catechism of the Catholic Church* as a source document for such programs. There is now a wealth of good material available, much of which is readily accessible on-line. These programs of catechesis can be promoted in dioceses, parishes, schools and universities.

Catechesis is intimately linked to evangelisation. Indeed, this is the way in which the Church speaks about catechesis. The revised *Directory for Catechesis* was promulgated in 2020. It explains that the catechetical journey develops "under the primacy of evangelisation" (Preface). It further states: "All Christian formation consists of entering more deeply into the kerygma". The word "kerygma", that is, the essential message of the Gospel, occurs frequently in the document. What the Directory is saying is that we need to ensure that the essential message of the Gospel is deeply embedded within all catechesis.

Given the contemporary situation in which many Catholics struggle to live the faith, the teaching of catechesis always seeks to nurture faith.

In the Apostolic Exhortation on "catechesis in our time", *Catechesi Tradendae* (1979), Pope St John Paul II described catechesis in these words,

> Within the whole process of evangelisation, the aim of catechesis is to be the teaching and maturation stage, that is to say, the period in which the Christian, having accepted by faith the person of Jesus Christ as the one Lord and having given Him complete adherence by sincere conversion of heart, endeavours to know better this Jesus to whom he has entrusted himself: to know His "mystery," the kingdom of God proclaimed by Him, the requirements and promises contained in His Gospel message, and the paths that He has laid down for anyone who wishes to follow Him. (*CT* 21)

Catholic schools

The primary responsibility for the education of children rests with their parents. This is a central part of Catholic teaching. However, this important role has come under significant attack in the culture. With an increasing number of households where both parents are in paid work there is little time left for them to take a foundational role in the education and formation of their children.

Properly understood, the role of the Catholic school is not to be supported by parents, but the other way around. The role of the Catholic school is to support the work of the parents in educating their children.

We have much work to do to addressing what has become an inverse relationship. It is imperative that the Church seeks new and better ways to support parents in educating their children and restoring their role as the primary educators and formers of their children. It must be the parents and not the children's peers who have the most significant influence in their human formation, in particular, the development of the Christian virtues.

Catholic schools offer the service of catechesis to assist parents in their task of forming their children in the faith.

The purpose of Catholic education is ultimately to assist young people in becoming disciples of Jesus Christ and living the sacramental life of the Church. Pope St John Paul II would not hesitate in saying that the Catholic school has the task of showing children how to become saints. This certainly involves the teaching of the basics of reading, writing and arithmetic, but is far more than this.

If our young people coming out of a Catholic education have not been presented with the full beauty and wonder of the Catholic faith in their human formation then we have not succeeded.

It is true that faith is a gift. It is a work of the Holy Spirit within the human heart. Catholic schools can no more 'produce' faithful Catholics than any of us can. But the Catholic school can provide the fullness of Catholic teaching that will provide the basis for faith to take root and grow, leading the young person to full Christian maturity.

Catholic Education takes as its mandate the mission Jesus entrusted to his Church to make disciples of all the nations (see Mt 28:19-20).

The achievement of our Catholic schools

From the beginnings of the Church in Australia, providing schools for the education of Catholic children has been a priority of both parents and pastors. We can rightly be proud of what has been accomplished over the past two hundred years.

Up to the first half the 20th century, Catholic schools were largely run by dedicated religious from various teaching orders. They lived and witnessed to deeply religious lives. They gave themselves totally to the Christian vocation of teaching which at its heart was Christian catechesis.

The second half of the century saw a decline in the number of members of religious orders and increased government funding for Catholic schools. Inevitably, lay staff began to replace the teaching religious. In the 1960s and 70s widespread debates about curriculum content and methods in religious education saw the rise of diocesan and school programs that were increasingly less comprehensive and less systematic, resulting in school graduates having less knowledge or understanding of the Catholic faith.

Coupled with this was a steep decline in participation in the sacraments and weekly attendance of Mass by families in their local parish. This was exacerbated by a general secularisation of contemporary Australian society that saw mainstream religious belief being challenged by dominant secular elites in academia and the media. The popular entertainment culture rejected moral constraints, emphasised sexual freedom and self-determination. This was accompanied by the radicalisation of moral and cultural beliefs and increasing incursions by government into private rights and freedoms.

By the early decades of the 21st century, researchers noted that the belief patterns of Catholic teachers were more or less the same as those of their non-religious peers in State schools. At the same time the Church's requirement for quality catechesis and religious formation remained in full force. In practice, this meant that cohorts of teachers, unformed in Catholic belief and practice, were being expected to sustain a program of evangelisation and Christian witness that they were simply incapable of delivering.

Now it is rare to find a cohort of teachers in a Catholic school who are practising or living their Catholic faith with any degree of regularity or commitment. This can, quite rightly, be described as an existential crisis: no longer are the systems and schools able to carry out their essential mission.

However, it is also true that there is extraordinary opportunity for the Church and its essential mission of evangelisation. Parents, including many who are not Catholic, want their children to have what the Catholic schools offer. Students and teachers continue to turn up for school every day, and Catholic schools continue the work of education, even though the curriculum may be becoming ever more secular.

There remains a deep reservoir of good will in the Catholic school system in Australia. By and large, it is staffed by well-meaning teachers who try to fulfil their mission, one which they may only partly understand. If our schools are to become, again, a well-spring of Catholic faith, if we are to build for a long-term resurgence of evangelisation and witness, then our schools and systems need to refocus on certain, explicit, essential commitments.

Focus on the Person of Jesus Christ

Every school needs to ensure that its key focus is the person of Jesus Christ. The explicit aim of the Catholic school is to bring Christ to our students and bring students to Christ. Thus, the Catholic school engages directly in the mission of the Church which is to bring the person and teaching of Christ to the world.

To achieve this the school staff need one-on-one help to enable them grow in their personal relationship with Jesus Christ. The Catholic school needs to provide direct opportunities for teachers to have their own encounter with Christ. A Catholic school will not just focus on the transmission of the faith to the students, but will also develop means by which the staff can come to real and personal faith.

For those in leadership in the school everything that the school does needs to be Christocentric. The leader in a Catholic school needs to be committed to the faith, be sacramentally active, and dedicated to advancing the faith within the school community.

Schools need to be as Catholic as they can

It must be the policy of the school to increase its portion of the staff who are practising Catholics. This will mean actively seeking out men and women of faith who want to advance the evangelising mission of the school. Catholic schools need to proactively promote the role of the teacher as one who can inspire young people to become disciples of Jesus Christ. This vision of the true goal of Catholic education inspired young people to join religious orders in the past. Under the right circumstances, young Catholics who are serious about their faith can be attracted to become teachers in our Catholic schools, and embrace this as their life's mission. It should be the case that only practising Catholic teachers are able to give religious instruction. If a school does not have sufficient such teachers, then one or more teachers who are committed to the faith should become the official catechists in the school and provide the religious instruction.

Every school needs competent and spiritually engaged staff. Every Catholic school should have or establish programs of on-going formation on the Catholic faith for all staff – Catholic or not.

It is essential that Catholic schools recruit principals and senior leaders who have an evangelising heart, who embrace and live their faith completely, and who are prepared to expect the same of their peers. The choice of leaders in Catholic education is critical to its future.

A visible Catholic culture

At the heart of the promotion of a Catholic culture in the school will be the provision of sound religious texts which reflect the full breadth and depth of the Catholic faith. Every student, Catholic or not, should develop a Catholic literacy and be exposed to the best Catholic imagery.

Every school needs curricula, statues, icons and crucifixes that project its Catholic identity. The Catholic school can readily draw on the rich patrimony of Catholic art, architecture, music and literature in all learning spaces and learning programs. It can integrate the "Catholic Curriculum" into every school subject. It can encourage students in the acquisition of artistic, literary, musical and performance skills at the service of the Church.

A Eucharistic culture

Every school needs to develop a Eucharistic culture. Thus, the school will encourage personal devotion and the living of a sacramental life. Regular class and school Masses are essential. Students should be familiar with their local parish church. They should be immersed in the liturgical year.

The school needs to provide regular opportunities, not only for students, but also for staff, to participate in Mass and Eucharistic worship. Catechesis on the sacraments should help deepen a sacramental understanding of Catholic life.

Wherever possible the Catholic school should provide a chapel with students and staff encouraged to visit it regularly.

A systematic curriculum

Every school needs a systematic curriculum of Catholic belief and practice for every year level. This curriculum needs to be supported by good theological texts which students can access.

Schools are places of intellectual life and growth, and so the religious curriculum needs to rival all the other subjects in scope, rigour and beauty. Senior school students should have a Catholic studies program which is intellectually challenging, opening them to the richness of the Catholic intellectual tradition.

All social outreach programs should be grounded in the full theological breadth and richness of Catholic social teaching and not become merely political action or shaped by passing ideological trends.

Students should be exposed to the witness and example of the great saints and martyrs. Saints can become the role models that inspire the students.

Oriented towards parish life

Every Catholic school needs to orient itself to its local parish. Thus, parish clergy should be welcomed any time in the school and see themselves as indispensable members of staff. The liturgical life of the school is oriented entirely to the parish cycle of worship. Each school should have a member of staff appointed as school/parish liaison, committed to building relationships between each school family and their parish.

University apostolate

Following on from the work of Catholic schools it is important that each diocese has a clear plan and commitment to supporting the faith of university students on campus. The years at university are very formative and it is a time when many young people are seeking the answers to life's most important questions. The intellectual environment often stimulates their quest for the truth both material and spiritual.

It is important that every university campus has an active Catholic society supported by campus ministers, and ideally a dedicated campus chaplain. University students should be able to have a place where they can meet with other Catholics, regularly attend Mass and adoration, pray the Rosary, bible studies, or courses on key aspects of the faith. It is through these particular offerings, sacramental, devotional and intellectual, that many Catholic students come to a point of personal commitment to the faith.

University ministry, which has been unapologetically Catholic, has proven to be very fruitful, resulting not only in a number of Catholic students returning to the practice of their faith but also producing a number of converts to the faith. Such campus ministries have also resulted in vocations to priesthood and religious life.

Campus ministry, solidly based in the Catholic faith, can be very fruitful, raising up young people who are strong in their faith and who love the Church. Many go on to become active in the ministry of the Church.

Order of catechist

There is a need at this time to reconsider the role of the catechist in the mission and ministry of the Church. Pope Francis in his Apostolic Letter, *Antiquum Ministerium*, instituting the Ministry of Catechist (2021), has alerted the Church to the important role the catechist plays in the handing on of the faith. He has invited episcopal conferences to find effective ways to establish a stable ministry of catechist in dioceses (*AM* 9).

One possible way forward is to institute an "Order of Catechists" within a diocese. Candidates for this ministry would understand that they have a vocation to teach and hand on the faith. They would receive a program of formation which may run for several years, and, when sufficiently formed, be mandated by the bishop. Such catechists are then installed in what is a stable and permanent ministry in the diocese.

Such catechists would perform their ministry within the parish under the guidance of the parish priest. They could help prepare parents who present their children for baptism. They would be the catechists for the RCIA. They would prepare children for the Sacraments of Initiation. They could have a role in offering adult catechesis, like Lenten programs, Scripture study and so on.

Providing systematic catechesis at the local parish level opens up new possibilities for parishes to be active agents of advancing catechesis as part of their evangelising mission.

Faith formation

The concept of faith formation has been raised often in the listening process leading up to the Plenary Council. This is clearly a recognised need felt by many in the Church.

Forming Catholics soundly in the faith should be one of the more important initiatives identified and implemented as a fruit of the deliberations of the Plenary Council. This can be a moment in which a renewal of catechesis will revitalise the faith of many Catholics. Freshly inspired by the beauty and truth of the faith of the Church they will become more confident advocates of and witnesses to the faith within their sphere of influence. They will become true missionary disciples advancing the Christian faith, not only within the Church, but more broadly within the society.

6

Understanding the Nature of the Church

In addition to the societal changes that we have spoken about we have also witnessed significant changes across the landscape of the Church over recent decades. Many of the changes have been the subject of much discussion and indeed anguish – from declining Mass attendance, the decrease in vocations, to the alienation of youth.

At the same time the Catholic Church has become the largest religious denomination in the country. Around one in five Australians identify as Catholic. However, we have now experienced for the first time in our history a decline in the number of people identifying as Catholic. The religious character of our nation is changing with those professing no religion now comprising the single largest grouping, at 30% of the population. Still, on a Sunday there are some 623,000 Catholics attending Mass, 11.8% of the Catholic population.

The Church has been deeply affected by revelations of sexual abuse by clergy and religious. The standing of the Church in the broader society has been diminished, and many members of the Church have had their trust in the Church greatly affected. This has been a very difficult time for all Catholics. It has no doubt contributed to a decline in identification with the Church among many.

Responding to the times

The Church must find its place amid a rapidly changing culture. It has to address the issue of decline of Christian faith within the culture and within its own ranks. There needs to be a serious reconsideration of how we envisage the mission of the Church. While we always wish to co-operate with those of good will to advance the good of humanity, we need to be aware that many now insist that the Church embrace the dominant values being espoused in the society, values which are at variance with our understanding of the nature of the human person and God's plan for human life.

We are justifiably proud of our contribution to Australian society in areas like health and aged care, service to the disadvantaged and in education. In Australia the Catholic Church is the most significant supplier of services in these areas outside the government itself. However, we need to be free to carry out our mission in these areas without being required to abandon our core understanding of the nature of the human person and the origin and destiny of each individual.

The Church's mission is essentially spiritual in nature. While Christian charity prompts our outreach to those in need, our goal is not merely the human advancement of society, but ultimately the eternal salvation of every person.

Pope Francis has warned on a number of occasions that the Church must not simply become another NGO (non-government organisation). When speaking to the Swiss Bishops on 1 December 2014 he said, "Your country has a long Christian tradition. You have a great and beautiful responsibility to maintain a living faith in your land." He added, "Without a living faith in the risen Christ, your beautiful churches and monasteries will gradually become museums; all the commendable works and institutions will lose their soul, leaving behind only empty spaces and abandoned people."

Encouraging the bishops to foster the faith of the people, he said, "The testimony of Christians and of parish communities can truly light the way and support their aspiration to happiness. In this way, the Church in Switzerland will be more clearly itself, the body of Christ and the people of God, and not only a beautiful organisation" (Address to Swiss Bishops, 1 December 2014).

In a letter written to the "People of God in Germany", in July 2019, Pope Francis urged the Church in Germany to build up the people and "not a perfectly organised and functioning NGO".

Understanding the nature of the Church

As the Church seeks to address the pastoral challenges it faces, one of the important issues will be the ability to define its inner nature and its essential mission with clarity. This clarity can be achieved by a return to the sources – the Scriptures, the Tradition, and settled magisterial teaching found in the *Catechism of the Catholic Church*. The Dogmatic Constitution on the Church, *Lumen Gentium*, is central to the way in which the Church in our time understands itself and should guide all reflection on the nature and role of the Church in the modern world.

Catholic theology, following the teaching of the Sacred Scriptures, emphasises that the Church is the Body of Christ, and Christ is its head. The *Catechism of the Catholic Church* explains that the Church "lives from him, in him, and for him; he lives with her and in her" (*CCC* 807). The relationship of Christ to the Church is expressed in the image of the head and its relationship with the body.

The head directs a body. The body needs the head, but the head needs the body to carry out its purposes.

Scripture says that God gave Jesus "as head over all things to the Church, which is his body" (Eph 1:22-23). Thus, the Church always looks to Christ and understands that there is a mystical union with him. Any movement of reform can always be tested to see if it brings the Church closer to Christ and ensures that Christ more effectively animates its life and mission.

There is a tendency abroad today to view the Church solely as a human institution, an international corporation, and to see its mission enshrined in its many good works. Against this tendency to see the Church merely in terms of its external reality it is necessary to emphasise the inner spiritual reality of the Church. What is important is that we are able to identify the soul of the Church.

St Augustine, in a sermon, spoke of the Holy Spirit as the soul of the Church: "What the soul is for the body of man, that the Holy Spirit is for the body of Christ, that is, the Church. The Holy Spirit operates in the whole Church that which the soul operates in the members of the one body" (*Sermones* 267.4). The Fathers of the Church spoke of the inner principle that generates the vitality and efficacy of the Church. St Irenaeus of Lyons, quoted in the *Catechism of the Catholic Church*, said: "Indeed, it is to the Church herself that the 'Gift of God' has been entrusted. . . . In it is in her that communion with Christ has been deposited, that is to say: the Holy Spirit, the pledge of incorruptibility, the strengthening of our faith and the ladder of our ascent to God. ... For where the Church is, there also is God's Spirit; where God's Spirit is, there is the Church and every grace" (*Adv. haeres.* 3,24,1).

Pope Pius XII wrote a significant encyclical on the nature of the

Church, entitled *Mystici Corporis Christi*, The Mystical Body of Christ (1943), where he said that the Holy Spirit is "the principle of every supernatural act in all parts of the Body" (*MCC* 57). The Church needs to be seen and understood as being animated by the Holy Spirit.

Once the mystery of the Church is recognised then one sees its nature and mission as being animated by the Holy Spirit. All efforts to renew the Church need to be guided by whether these efforts are actually animated by the Holy Spirit. This must be the test for all renewal.

Preparation for the Plenary Council

The Church in Australia will hold the first of two sessions of a Plenary Council in October 2021. It has been over 80 years since the last Plenary Council, which was held in 1937. Preparation for this significant ecclesial event included an extensive program of consultation conducted in 2019. Catholics were asked, "What do you think God is asking of us at this time?"

The consultation revealed that Catholics desire a church that is open and welcoming. There was a concern to reach out in acceptance of all people, especially those on the margins – Australia's First Peoples, the poor and disadvantaged, and those whose lives are at variance from Church teaching. While this showed admirable human concern for those who are struggling in one way or another, there was not much focus on the need to advance the spiritual mission of the Church, especially in its mission to bring Christ to people.

When it came to articulating the mission of the Church it seemed that one of the most popular concerns was for action to save the environment. Some submissions urged the Church to modernise its teachings so that it was more in tune with the contemporary world. Issues like the inclusion of divorced and remarried Catholics received attention as did recognition of need for inclusion of those with same-sex attraction.

Papers were prepared around a number of themes. What soon became apparent was the lack of a sense of urgency to proclaim Christ to a nation that is losing adherence to the Christian faith. There appeared little appreciation in the submissions of the serious threats to Catholic life that were emerging in the culture.

There was a good deal of emphasis on the need for the Church to be welcoming. However, there was no reference to the requirement for a 'welcomed' person to address any areas where their life or attitudes which are not aligned with the teaching of the Church. The Lord warns us that not all who call out "Lord, Lord" will enter the Kingdom of God, but "He who does the will of my Father who is in heaven" (Mt 7:21). Jesus expects conversion of heart and of manner of life to be a pre-requisite for entry into His Kingdom.

There was a good deal of emphasis too on the need for the Church to listen. But to whom? While the Church needs to listen to the concerns of people it must first listen to the Lord. In being called by the Lord to "make disciples" (Mt 28:19) we are reminded that our basic disposition is one of listening to the Lord. A disciple is one who submits heart and soul to the teaching given by Christ, now through the Church. St Paul warned the Roman community: "Do not be conformed to this world, but be transformed by the renewal of your mind" (Rom 12:2).

With the culture around us changing so rapidly and the pressures to conform becoming so great this message is very important. St Paul says a similar thing to the Ephesians, "be renewed in the spirit of your minds" (Eph 4:23). The time is fast approaching when each Catholic will need to decide whether to go the way of Christ or choose to follow the prevailing culture. There can be no middle ground. It will not be unlike the situation of the first Christians where they had to choose to stand out against the culture and risk what may befall them. They knew that Christ offered the path to eternal life and so if sacrifice was required it would be accepted. Jesus had no illusions about this: "... and he who does not take up his cross and follow me is not worthy of me" (Mt 10:38).

While many hopes were expressed for a future Church living out and witnessing to the Catholic faith, the impression from the consultation process is one of reducing the Church to the human or horizontal level, desiring that the Church conform itself more to the prevailing culture.

Governance review

In 2019, in the light of the Royal Commission into Institutional Response to Child Sexual Abuse, the Australian bishops commissioned a review of governance in the Catholic Church in Australia. The draft report, entitled *The Light from the Southern Cross, Co-Responsible Governance in the Catholic Church in Australia*, proposed 86 recommendations. Before the bishops even had the opportunity to consider the report it was leaked to the media. Once the bishops had a chance to discuss the report at the May 2020 Bishops' Plenary in June 2020, they published their response.

While appreciative of the work done and the many recommendations made, the bishops identified some serious flaws in the report. The bishops noted that in the report the Church was presented primarily in terms of only one of its dimensions – that of the People of God. While this description of the Church was used in the teachings of the Second Vatican Council, it is only one way of viewing the nature of the Church. The governance review put significant emphasis on this concept and failed to capture the full mystery of the Church as taught by the Council. It can give the impression that the Church is primarily human in character and Church governance should be more democratic in structure.

The document on the Church, *Lumen Gentium*, in fact, devotes a chapter (Chapter 3) to the question of the hierarchical nature of the Church. It is entitled, "On the Hierarchical Structure of the Church and in particular on the Episcopate". It gives considerable attention to the role of the bishop in governing the local Church:

> Bishops, therefore, with their helpers, the priests and deacons, have taken up the service of the community, presiding in place of God over the flock, whose shepherds they are, as teachers for doctrine, priests for sacred worship, and ministers for governing. And just as the office granted individually to Peter, the first among the apostles, is permanent and is to be transmitted to his successors, so also the apostles' office of nurturing the Church is permanent, and is to be exercised without interruption by the sacred order of bishops. Therefore, the Sacred Council teaches that bishops by divine institution have succeeded to the place of the apostles, as shepherds of the Church, and he who hears them, hears Christ, and he who rejects them, rejects Christ and Him who sent Christ. (*LG* 20)

The Church by her very nature is hierarchical and is not democratic.

The way people envisage the Church shapes the way in which they envisage its governance. The consultation process gave rise to many voices wanting increased participation by lay people in the governance of the Church. The Church has, in fact, provided many ways in which lay people have roles of governance and are involved directly in consultation with bishops.

The report fostered the idea of co-responsibility in the Church. This is a valid notion promoted in recent Church documents, however, it needs to be set within the sacramental economy of leadership. Co-responsibility understands that there are different gifts and roles within the Church, each with its own character, and able to contribute for the good of all as outlined in St Paul's teaching on the Church as the Body of Christ (see I Cor 12).

Bishops and priests exercise a governance role which includes three features (or *munera*) *teaching, sanctifying and governing*. To concentrate on one without recognising the interaction with the others diminishes the distinctive nature of leadership within the Church. Within the Church, governance cannot be separated from teaching and sanctifying. It is for this reason, based on the Lord's intention, that governance belongs to the ordained ministry.

The clergy, especially the diocesan clergy, have an immediate focus on the care of the Christian community (*ad intra*), the laity, in the mind of the Church, have an essential mission in the world (*ad extra*). Of course, all in the Church are called to mission, but the laity, living in the world, have a special role of being a Christian presence and witness within the society. It is important that there is not excessive interest in lay involvement in governance to the detriment of their presence and mission in the society.

On a number of occasions Pope Francis has warned lay Catholics against what he called, "sacristy Catholicism", that is, more interested in internal church matters than in a missionary orientation towards the world. In launching Missionary Month in October

2019 Pope Francis said, "Please, let us not live a sacristy faith" (Vespers address, 1 October 2019). He urged lay Catholics to be part of the Church 'on the go', that is, actively taking the Gospel to the world. "If it is not on the go, it is not Church," Pope Francis stressed. "A Church on the go, a missionary Church, is a Church that does not waste time lamenting things that go wrong, the loss of faithful, the values of the time now in the past." Pope Francis wants the lay faithful not to dwell on internal matters, but to embrace the call to evangelise.

Understanding the true nature of the Church

It is therefore critical that as the Church in Australia approaches the first session of the Plenary Council that all participants have a full and comprehensive understanding of the nature of the Church, and in particular appreciate that the nature of the Church cannot be changed. It was Jesus Christ who gave us the Church, his mystical bride. The Church is a gift, not our possession with which we can endlessly tinker and change. While there are always ways in which governance can be improved, and the Plenary Council can explore this, excessive attention to governance can distract from the more important issues facing the Church in our time.

7

The Pastoral Challenge

As we have been discussing, in the face of vast shifts in the culture, the Church in Australia has struggled to find its way. One image of describing the experience of the Church over the centuries is that of a boat, the Barque of Peter, swept by waves. The Scriptural reference is that of the storm on the Sea of Galilee (see Mt 8:23-27). The drama of this scene is captured wonderfully in the painting by Rembrandt. The medieval theologian, St Anselm, is quoted as saying, "The barque of the Church may be swept by the waves, but it can never sink because Christ is there." History has shown that the Church has endured all sorts of trials. However, at each new moment in history as new trials appear, the way of response can be difficult to navigate.

When confronted by seemingly unsolvable challenges, the human response can take various forms. It can choose not to face the challenges and carry on as before, 'business as usual'. Or a leader can erect a false hope that it will all eventually resolve itself. This can be reflected in the idea of the pendulum – it is swinging one way now but it will inevitably swing back. Or a leader may simply be paralysed by fear and choose not to address evident issues because they are just too hard.

In this historical moment, knowing that Christ is with us, we must take courage to face what is before us. What is important is that we are able to read the signs of the times correctly and then we act under divine guidance. For this is never just a human struggle. It is also true that the strength of faith flows in part from a confidence and trust in the Church where the Holy Spirit is truly active.

The confidence of the Church has no doubt been affected by revelations, not just of the extent of sexual abuse of children by Church personnel, but of the failure of Church leadership to confront the problem honestly and courageously. Efforts to push the issue to one side have done enormous harm, both to victims of sexual abuse as well as the moral authority of the Church. Awareness of past failure can however damage the confidence needed to deal with the issues we now face.

The effectiveness of our response is also diluted by the incursion of the cultural shifts into the hearts and minds of many Catholics. There are now many in the Church who will not accept some of the moral teachings of the Church. Some seek to minimise the demands of the Gospel and prefer a softer and less demanding message, avoiding the call to repentance which is at the heart of the message of Christ. Some reduce the Gospel to a reassuring humanism, avoiding the 'hard sayings' of Christ.

Priests know that there are many in their congregation who do not accept the Church's teaching on certain matters. Knowing this can lead those with pastoral leadership to avoid certain vital topics both in conversation and in formal teaching for fear of upsetting people and opening up difficult interchanges.

There is a very strong temptation to turn a blind eye to a range of immoral practices. To confront and correct error is extremely hard. Pastors, for the sake of peace and harmony, pass over false beliefs for fear of conflict or causing offence. Thus, pastoral inaction becomes the pattern. The prophetic edge of the Church is thus lost and Christian proclamation of truth is compromised.

It is argued that to frankly address these issues will cause dissension and division. Of course, the preacher needs to be charitable and humble in his presentation, but this cannot be the excuse for never touching sensitive topics. The Lord understood that division could result from his message, even within families: "Do you think that I have come to give peace on earth? No, I tell you, but rather division" (Lk 12:51).

St Paul's stirring admonition to Timothy is particularly relevant for us today:

> I charge you in the presence of God and of Christ Jesus who is to judge the living and the dead, and by his appearing and his kingdom, preach the word, be urgent in season and out of season, convince, rebuke, and exhort, be unfailing in patience and in teaching (2 Tim 4:1-2).

St Paul goes on to explain why such bold and zealous pastoral action is needed:

> For the time is coming when people will not endure sound teaching, but having itching ears they will accumulate for themselves teachers to suit their own likings and will turn away from listening to the truth and wander into myths (2 Tim 4:3-4).

Surely this is an apt description of the situation of the Church in Australia today. In an instruction, the Prophet Ezekiel is told that he is to be a watchman: "So you, son of man, I have made a watchman for the house of Israel: whenever you hear a word from my mouth, you shall give them a warning from me" (Ez 33:7). So too, every Christian leader has the role of being a watchman. Failure to carry out the role of watchman, we are warned, will be met with judgement from God because the failure is not just personal but is a failure to the people entrusted to them.

Judgement

A consistent theme in Sacred Scripture is that sin when unrepented leads to judgement. The Scriptures point to the judgement of God coming upon individuals and nations within human history. This is a powerful theme in the Old Testament, but echoed also with no less power in the New Testament. In the Book of Revelations, the messages to the seven churches contain clear warnings of judgement upon them unless they repent.

There are numerous instances of the prophets of the Old Testament warning of the judgement of God upon His people who have abandoned Him in idolatry or moral collapse. For example, the Prophet Ezekiel says that because Jerusalem has "wickedly rebelled against my ordinances" God says that He will "execute judgements in the midst of you" (see Ez 5:5-9).

Many times, the prophets have attributed the sufferings that descended upon the people to be the result of their sins. They were being chastised. The ultimate purpose of such judgement is not punishment, but purification and conversion. The time of exile led to the salutary realisation of the extent of sin in Israel. The Book of Lamentations records the depth of misery, but also the recognition of the cause: "Jerusalem sinned grievously" (Lam 1:8). From the depth of suffering came the heartfelt confession of sin and cry for forgiveness: "Hear, O Lord, and have mercy, for we have sinned before you" (see Baruch 3:1-8).

Sin has consequences. Sin brings suffering. St Paul says clearly, "The wages of sin is death" (Rom 6:23). As goodness begets movements of grace, so sin begets movements of evil. As whole societies become caught up in sin, the suffering across them becomes extensive. Abandonment of God is not morally neutral. It always has grave consequences.

The path of repentance

The Scriptures give us the antidote for sin. It is repentance. The individual Catholic knows that they need to confess their sins regularly and receive forgiveness through the Sacrament of Penance. The Catholic Catechism teaches, "Those who approach the sacrament of Penance obtain pardon from God's mercy for the offence committed against him, and are, at the same time, reconciled with the Church which they have wounded by their sins and which by charity, by example, and by prayer labours for their conversion" (*CCC* 1422).

When sin has corrupted a society, the repentance needs to take a communal form. We witness in the Old Testament spiritual leaders like Nehemiah leading the people in a communal act of repentance (see Neh 1:5-9). As the Church celebrated the arrival of the new millennium, Pope St John Paul II led the Church in an act of repentance. Recalling it in his encyclical *Novo Millennio Ineunte*, At the Beginning of the New Millennium (2001), the Pope commented:

> How could we forget the moving Liturgy of 12 March 2000 in Saint Peter's Basilica, at which, looking upon our Crucified Lord, I asked forgiveness in the name of the Church for the sins of all her children? This "purification of memory" has strengthened our steps for the journey towards the future and has made us more humble and vigilant in our acceptance of the Gospel (*NMI* 6).

The Christian cannot just seek forgiveness for personal sin, but can cry out for forgiveness on behalf of the broader society. At the heart of this cry for forgiveness is appealing to God's mercy. As Moses appealed to God more than once for mercy to be shown towards a headstrong people who had lapsed from faith (see Ex 32:30-33), so the Christian prays for mercy upon humanity, and upon societies abandoning truth and goodness.

As darkness grows, the urgency for our intercession increases. Christians cannot ignore the danger that is facing societies as they abandon God. We have a spiritual duty to pray for humanity. St Paul encourages the Christian faithful to pray for their societies and for those in leadership: "First of all, then, I urge that supplications, prayers, intercessions, and thanksgivings be made for all men, for kings and all who are in high positions, that we may lead a quiet and peaceful life, godly and respectful in every way" (1 Tim 2:1-2).

The Christian lives within human society and needs to pray constantly for the society and those in leadership so that, at least, we may be able to enjoy freedom and peace.

While speaking on the judgement of God it is also critically important to remember that at the same time our God is love. God created us in love to be in relationship with Him. His plan for humanity, expressed in the moral law, is a plan for happiness. In not preaching the truth of the moral law we are not only bringing judgement on ourselves but just as importantly we are denying the people a teaching which is the way to happiness and human fulfilment.

Calling to conversion

It is the responsibility of the Church to preach the full truth given to us by God. The human heart wants to know the truth, it desires the truth. As St Augustine said "the heart is restless until it rests in

God". To hold back from speaking the truth we are not being compassionate or 'more understanding', rather we are denying people the only way to authentic happiness and fulfilment.

The Plenary Council is an opportunity for the Church to declare its commitment to announcing the fullness of Christian teaching, not in a spirit of condemnation, but in a sincere desire to help people find the path to life and salvation. In doing this the Church invites people to conversion and also intercedes for human society, asking for mercy.

8

The Parish: a Missionary Focused Community

For the Catholic the normal and most natural way of living the faith is in and through the local parish community. The parish is the locus of the sacramental life. We are baptised in the parish church and receive the other sacraments of initiation (Confirmation and First Holy Communion) within the parish community. The parish community gathers on the Lord's Day to celebrate the Holy Eucharist, not just as a collection of individuals, but as brothers and sisters united in faith and a desire to live the Christian life.

The parish offers us an important source of Christian fellowship. Here we are in an environment where we are with those who share what is deepest within us, our faith. When we gather as a community we are encouraged by the example of faith and Christian living of those in the parish community. There is a silent and hidden, but very real bond, that unites us. We are brothers and sisters in the Lord.

We are nourished in our faith both by the sacraments as well as the preaching and catechesis that are offered to us through the parish.

In his Apostolic Exhortation, *Evangelii Gaudium*, Pope Francis expresses confidence in the future of the parish. He says, "The parish is not an outdated institution; precisely because it possesses great flexibility, it can assume quite different contours depending on the openness and missionary creativity of the pastor and the community" (*EG* 28). In other words, parishes can adapt to changed circumstances. Now is the time for such change. The Pope says that the parish is to be "a centre of constant missionary outreach" (ibid). To do this he says, "In all its activities the parish encourages and trains its members to be evangelisers" (ibid).

The Pope is presenting a new way of envisaging the spiritual and pastoral profile of a parish.

Placing the parish on a missionary footing

Priests are essentially trained to be pastors. They see their primary role as caring for their parish community. This will play out in the provision of sacramental opportunities, preparing people for receiving various sacraments, visiting the sick and infirm, and fostering a spirit of community among the parishioners.

The time has come for a new pastoral vision for priests. The Church is saying that priests are called to be evangelisers first and foremost. In a cultural situation where faith is declining at an increasing rate, the priest needs to re-orient his pastoral priorities. Evangelisation must now become the driving pastoral work of the priest.

In 2020 the Congregation for the Clergy released an Instruction entitled, "The pastoral conversion of the Parish community in the service of the evangelising mission of the Church" (PC). The Instruction speaks of the need for parishes to see themselves in a new way – they are to be "centres conducive to an encounter with Christ". Taking its lead from Pope Francis the document encourages parishes to seek new ways of "how best to proclaim the Gospel" (PC

1); the parish is to become "an evangelising community". The document calls on priests and lay parishioners to begin to re-imagine the parish.

And a warning is given, drawing again from the teaching of Pope Francis, "If the parish does not exude that spiritual dynamic of evangelisation, it runs the risk of becoming self-referential and fossilised, offering experiences that are devoid of evangelical flavour and missionary drive, of interest only to small groups" (PC 17).

All the works of the parish need to have an evangelical orientation. The document says, for instance, "Catechesis needs to be presented as an ongoing proclamation of the Mystery of Christ, the objective of which is to foster in the heart of the baptised that full stature of Christ (see Eph 4:13) that is derived from a personal encounter with the Lord of life" (PC 23).

In the Australian context the diminishing numbers of people participating in the sacramental life of the Church is a compelling reason itself to adopt this path urgently.

Pastoral conversion

The phrase constantly used in the document is "pastoral conversion". How can such a conversion occur?

We have witnessed in recent years the example of some parishes which have been able to go down the path of pastoral conversion. Central to their ability to effect this change in orientation is firstly to be found in the pastoral leadership – the clergy and some key parishioners. The parish leadership have embraced the need for a pastoral conversion in the way the ministry of the parish is carried out. They have begun to plan for a new way of being parish, centred on developing a missionary dynamic.

The second element is a change in the focus of preaching. The Sunday homily needs to become evangelistic, calling people to faith.

Thirdly, the parish needs to offer opportunities for a personal encounter with Christ. This often takes the form of programs which have evangelisation at their heart. There are now many suitable programs and initiatives available to assist a parish community. Parish leaders do not have to invent things themselves. One of the great advances available to us now is to use online presentations of Catholic evangelical preaching and teachings. All a parish needs to do is to set up opportunities for people to gather to listen to great Catholic material. These can be offered during the week or on weekends.

Coupled with such programs should be regular parish missions and organising of guest speakers who have gifts in evangelical preaching and teaching. Each parish should have a parish mission lasting one week at least once a year. A mission reinvigorates the faith of the parishioners, builds community and offers the opportunity for those outside the community to hear the Gospel. A key component of a mission is the opportunity for the Sacrament of Penance, especially through the ministry of a visiting priest.

Various forms of outreach activities which involve evangelistic preaching and teaching can become a regular feature of parish life. Such events can also be opportunities to reach out to parents of children attending Catholic schools. Many are disengaged with the parish but do have an awareness of the value of the faith, at least for their children. Our schools offer access to many who have a Catholic heritage and to others who are well disposed towards the Catholic faith. Parents in our schools are a natural group to reach out to and invite to participate in evangelisation activities.

There is value in recommending and providing parishioners

with the opportunity for retreats which seek to renew and inflame their faith.

The Catholic people sense a need for further formation in the faith and in the Christian life (this was evident in the consultation for the Plenary Council). Diocesan programs can be implemented within the parish, or parishioners encouraged to engage with the many programs now available online.

The parish needs to form those who are drawn to Christ in a new way. Programs of catechesis, Scripture study groups, prayer groups all offer ongoing formation and support. The formation of small groups is a proven way to foster personal spiritual growth. Every group, though, needs to foster an outward-looking orientation. They need to seek to draw others into their group, avoiding becoming closed and self-referential.

To embark on this process of pastoral conversion will not be easy as many parishes are quite set in their ways. Also, embracing this path will require much patience. Seeking quick results to confirm the value of this approach will lead to disappointment. A parish will need to adopt a course and hold steady on this path for many years. The results may be slow in coming, but come they will. This will not be the outcome of human effort alone, but ultimately it will be the fruit of the action of the grace of God.

Evangelisation and the Holy Spirit

The work of evangelisation is not a human enterprise, it is a work of God, a work of the Holy Spirit. In his great document on evangelisation, *Evangelii Nuntiandi*, Proclaiming the Gospel (1975), Pope St Paul VI devoted a lengthy reflection on the role of the Holy Spirit in the life of Jesus and in the life of the early Church and then spoke of the critical role the Holy Spirit plays in the work of evangelisation today. The whole passage given in #75 of the Apostolic Exhortation deserves quoting, but here we can offer some of the key insights.

Pope Paul VI has as his opening statement: "Evangelisation will never be possible without the action of the Holy Spirit" (*EN* 75). In speaking about the life of the Church the Pope makes the important statement: "The Holy Spirit is the soul of the Church". This reminds us that the Church is not just a human enterprise, but is a work of God. At the heart of the Church is divine life, mediated through the indwelling Spirit. He then says,

> It is He who explains to the faithful the deep meaning of the teaching of Jesus and of His mystery. It is the Holy Spirit who, today just as at the beginning of the Church, acts in every evangeliser who allows himself to be possessed and led by Him. The Holy Spirit places on his lips the words which he could not find by himself, and at the same time the Holy Spirit predisposes the soul of the hearer to be open and receptive to the Good News and to the kingdom being proclaimed.

It is the Holy Spirit who inspires the evangeliser and the Holy Spirit who moves in the heart of the listener.

Pope St Paul VI understands that efforts at evangelisation which are manufactured at the human level alone will never be fruitful:

> Techniques of evangelisation are good, but even the most advanced ones could not replace the gentle action of the Spirit. The most perfect preparation of the evangeliser has no effect without the Holy Spirit. Without the Holy Spirit the most convincing dialectic has no power over the heart of man. Without Him the most highly developed schemas resting on a sociological or psychological basis are quickly seen to be quite valueless.

The Pope then makes an interesting comment, suggesting that

he is seeing a new movement of the Holy Spirit, akin to what happened at Pentecost: "We live in the Church at a privileged moment of the Spirit".

Finally, he summarises his thought:

> It must be said that the Holy Spirit is the principal agent of evangelisation: it is He who impels each individual to proclaim the Gospel, and it is He who in the depths of consciences causes the word of salvation to be accepted and understood. But it can equally be said that He is the goal of evangelisation: He alone stirs up the new creation, the new humanity of which evangelisation is to be the result, with that unity in variety which evangelisation wishes to achieve within the Christian community. Through the Holy Spirit the Gospel penetrates to the heart of the world, for it is He who causes people to discern the signs of the times- signs willed by God- which evangelisation reveals and puts to use within history.

As the Church responds now to the call for a new evangelising movement at the heart of her mission, the place to begin will be to invoke the Holy Spirit. No evangelisation will be fruitful unless those involved are submissive to the Spirit. This will mean deep prayer and discernment. It will require sensitivity to the promptings of the Spirit. It will be fruitful to the extent that the Holy Spirit is present and active.

So, Pope Paul VI concludes: "We exhort all evangelisers, whoever they may be, to pray without ceasing to the Holy Spirit with faith and fervour and to let themselves prudently be guided by Him as the decisive inspirer of their plans, their initiatives and their evangelising activity".

Pope Paul VI ushered in a new vision for the evangelising mission of the Church. His words still inspire today and can stir our hearts with a desire to be filled with evangelising zeal.

> Let us therefore preserve our fervour of spirit. Let us preserve the delightful and comforting joy of evangelising, even when it is in tears that we must sow. May it mean for us – as it did for John the Baptist, for Peter and Paul, for the other apostles and for a multitude of splendid evangelisers all through the Church's history – an interior enthusiasm that nobody and nothing can quench. May it be the great joy of our consecrated lives. And may the world of our time, which is searching, sometimes with anguish, sometimes with hope, be enabled to receive the Good News not from evangelisers who are dejected, discouraged, impatient or anxious, but from ministers of the Gospel whose lives glow with fervour, who have first received the joy of Christ, and who are willing to risk their lives so that the kingdom may be proclaimed and the Church established in the midst of the world. (*EN* 80)

Evangelical preaching

To effectively revitalise a parish and move it from being a parish offering pastoral services to a parish with a missionary intent, the role of preaching is of vital importance. The key locus for preaching, of course, is the Sunday sermon, but if the parish develops evangelical programs then the preaching in them is also of importance.

Evangelical preaching has as its core purpose fostering conversion and eliciting faith. A preacher can examine himself as to whether this was the focus of the sermon he just preached. While preaching may involve some exegesis or offering some spiritual or moral ideals, it must move to another level.

As noted above, preaching must be 'in the Spirit'. Preparation for preaching should involve invoking the guidance and inspiration of the Holy Spirit. The words of Pope St Paul VI quoted above should guide the preacher as he prepares: "The most perfect preparation of the evangeliser has no effect without the Holy Spirit" (*EN* 75). Indeed, preaching should witness to the fire of the Spirit animating the preaching. The Lord declared: "I came to cast fire on the earth and would that it were already kindled" (Lk 12:49). It was with tongues of fire that the Holy Spirit came upon the Apostles at Pentecost.

The content of the preaching, inspired by the texts of Scripture and the liturgical season or feast, should be on salvation found in Jesus Christ. Pope St Paul VI, in describing the content of the message, turns first to the message of Jesus himself which he summarises in these words, "As the kernel and centre of His Good News, Christ proclaims salvation, this great gift of God which is liberation from everything that oppresses man but which is above all liberation from sin and the Evil One, in the joy of knowing God and being known by Him, of seeing Him, and of being given over to Him" (*EN* 9). He adds, "This kingdom and this salvation, which are the key words of Jesus Christ's evangelisation, are available to every human being as grace and mercy" (*EN* 10).

St Paul, the great evangelist, offers a very clear insight into his understanding of the nature of Christian preaching when he writes in I Corinthians: "For the Jews demand signs and Greeks seek wisdom, but we preach a crucified Christ" (I Cor 1:22-23). Paul understood that preaching Christ crucified was viewed as "folly" by many, but his experience had shown him that it was the power of God to save (see I Cor 1:18).

Preaching to the regular parish community on a Sunday should seek to call forth a personal response in faith. People should leave the Mass on Sunday inspired to live the Christian life with more fervour and commitment. Preaching within the Liturgy should be complemented by other more informal settings like a mission evening. These settings offer an opportunity for more personal response. Evangelical preaching should be oriented towards such response. We saw that when Peter preached at Pentecost his listeners asked, "What must we do brothers?" (see Acts 2:37). People need a means whereby they can respond.

What is needed here is an opportunity for personal prayer. A person deeply convinced of the need to embrace faith in Christ can be led through a prayer of repentance and acceptance of Christ as their Lord and Saviour. Others may just wish to open their hearts to God to receive his grace or healing. Provision of opportunities for individual ministry to people is an important component to evangelical preaching. It is often the moment of personal prayer that becomes the means by which their soul is flooded with divine grace and they are changed. They have tasted the saving love and mercy of God.

Another element in the development of evangelical preaching is the role that music plays. It is time to examine the quality of the music in the Sunday Mass. Music is a very important means of lifting hearts and minds to the worship of God. Music in the Liturgy should have worship of God as its central purpose and so care should be taken in the choice of music. The music should stir the soul and for this to happen it is important that musicians and singers are themselves offering worship to God as they serve the community.

In more informal settings the use of music which inspires openness to God helps create a stronger atmosphere of faith in which the preaching can be done. Contemporary "Praise and Worship" music is very conducive to fostering an atmosphere of expectant faith laying the foundations for response to evangelical preaching.

The development of evangelical preaching is a key component in the pastoral conversion called for by the Church.

The new movements and the parish

The stirring vision of Pope St Paul VI was not without its providential realisation in the Church of recent times. In the years following the Council there was a spiritual springtime as new expressions of evangelical fervour emerged within the Church. This evangelical fervour emerged particularly among lay men and women who have formed themselves into new ecclesial communities or movements.

One person who recognised their significance for the future of the Church was Pope St John Paul II who actively sought to encourage them and bring them into the very heart of the Church. In his Apostolic Exhortation on the role of the lay person in the Church and in the world, *Christifideles Laici* (1988), he affirmed their importance for advancing the mission of the Church, especially by engaging with and reaching out to the society in which they found themselves.

These diverse groups have certain common characteristics that would seem necessary for the establishment of an ecclesial community. With some exceptions, the key characteristics of these movements are:

- They have a founder whose particular charism gave birth to the movement.
- They are predominantly, but not exclusively, composed of lay persons.

- They develop a certain ecclesial structure and communal expression.
- They develop a set of teachings and methods that express the movement's charism.
- They have an explicit commitment to evangelise.

While these new expressions of Catholic life have distinct characteristics they follow in a long tradition of groups, associations and communities that have arisen during the two millennia of Christianity. The history of the Church witnesses to many diverse ways in which the Holy Spirit has stirred up spiritual movements which are capable of meeting the specific needs of the time, often when the institutional Church has struggled to address new challenges to its mission. We can consider here various monastic and mendicant orders, confraternities, sodalities, charitable and educational societies, social welfare organisations, and Catholic Action groups. In the modern period, and due largely to the encouragement of the Second Vatican Council, the ecclesial movements represent "a new era of group endeavours of the lay faithful" (*CL* 29).

Members of these new movements, while wishing to embrace the charism and the community life of the movement, see themselves at the service of the Church. They desire to assist in the renewal of the Church and are willing to assist in the spiritual regeneration of parish life.

A wise pastor will seek to engage members of these movements in the mission of his parish. He will do this while respecting the charism of the movement. The wise pastor will work with members in a spirit of co-responsibility for the mission of the Church. On their part members of an ecclesial movement will serve the parish without seeking to advance its own cause alone.

Pastoral conversion

The pastoral conversion called for in parish communities is not beyond possibility. While many parishes are very settled in their way of operating, the times call for change; the Church calls for change. We cannot just be parish as we have always been. Conversion is a work of grace so a priest can gather with a small group of parishioners and pray for the grace to become a missionary community. What may seem humanly impossible is always possible under grace.

The Plenary Council is an ideal opportunity for this understanding of being parish to be established as the new path for all parish communities in Australia. The Plenary Council can launch a new springtime for parish life grounded in missionary orientation.

9

SIGNS OF HOPE

When we look to the future of our society and of the Church naturally we wonder which way things will go. The Christian looks to the future with the virtue of hope. This hope in not in ourselves and how we can shape the future, though we have a role to play. Despite the many challenges that we encounter we know that Christ has been victorious. Light will triumph over darkness, and life will triumph over death.

Despite the tenor of the Lord's predictions that times of severe trial are coming, the Lord assured his disciples that the final coming of the Lord will be a moment of triumph for those who have been faithful: "And then they will see the Son of man coming in a cloud with power and great glory. Now when these things begin to take place, look up and raise your heads, because your redemption is drawing near" (Lk 21:27-28).

However, Christian hope can be severely tested at this time and our immediate future as Catholics may be difficult indeed. In 2005, speaking to Mexican bishops on their 'ad limina' visit to Rome Pope Benedict said,

> Confronted by today's changing and complex panorama, the virtue of hope is subject to harsh trials in the community of believers. For this very reason, we must be apostles

who are filled with hope and joyful trust in God's promises. God never abandons his people; indeed, he invites them to conversion so that his Kingdom may become a reality. The Kingdom of God does not only mean that God exists, that he is alive, but also that he is present and active in the world.

Pope Benedict XVI devoted his second encyclical, *Spes Salvi* (2007), to the theme of Christian hope. The Pope from the outset declared that Christian faith is based on the consciousness that we have been saved. This salvation is offered to us, the Pope says, "in the sense that we have been given hope, trustworthy hope, by virtue of which we can face our present: the present, even if it is arduous, can be lived and accepted if it leads towards a goal, if we can be sure of this goal, and if it is great enough to justify the effort of the journey" (*SS* 1).

Christian hope, grounded as it is in divine revelation, opens our minds to see things beyond what is immediately and tangibly evident: "... the Gospel is not merely a communication of things that can be known – it is one that makes things happen and is life-changing. The dark door of time, of the future, has been thrown open. The one who has hope lives differently; the one who hopes has been granted the gift of a new life" (*SS* 2).

The Christian lives always in hope. No matter how dark things may become, how hopeless the situation may seem, the Christian lifts his/her head and looks to the skies, because from there will come the Saviour. Thus, Christians never despair or allow themselves to be overcome by fear. Buoyed by hope, they battle on in the knowledge that in the end "all will be well" (Julian of Norwich).

Chapter 11 of the Letter to the Hebrews is a meditation on the nature of Christian hope. Faith enables hope, it says, and provides "a conviction of things not seen" (Heb 11:1). The chapter then lists a number of Old Testament figures whose lives were characterised by living faith. The Letter comments, "These all died in faith, not having received what was promised" (Heb 11:13). It is often true that a person of deep faith and courageous conviction who has laboured long and hard may not see the outcome of their efforts, even their life's work. But they have not laboured in vain. The Lord commented that one plants and another reaps (see Jn 4:37).

It may well be that a life of dedicated service in the cause of the Gospel may not reveal evident fruits, but what is important is that one has been faithful to what has been expected. St Peter Chanel laboured hard on the island of Fortuna in the Pacific. He was martyred and shortly after the whole island converted to the Catholic faith. Mother Teresa of Calcutta is quoted as saying, "God does not require that we be successful only that we be faithful." It becomes possible to do this when our faith in animated by Christian hope.

The Christian also knows that this world is not the final place for us. A Christian lives in hope of heaven, our true homeland. The author of the Letter to the Hebrews comments as such when he says that those who laboured in hope sensed that fruitfulness would come, "having seen it and greeted it from afar" (Heb 11:13). They were striving for a homeland, he says. This homeland they saw from afar, knowing that they were strangers and exiles on earth.

Christians have their homeland in heaven and await the coming of the Lord. Here on earth they strive with hope, knowing that even if the outcome of their striving is not revealed, they have a destiny of glory that awaits them. This means that Christians will engage with the struggles and challenges of the times, but are not condemned to find value in their life's work simply in terms of human achievement.

Signs of hope

As we face many challenges we are encouraged by some signs of hope, even if they are small, faint lights amid the growing darkness.

Thus, it is encouraging to see a new generation of young Catholics arising. These are young people with a fresh vision of being Christian, an evident love of the Church and want to embrace and engage in its mission.

A distinguishing characteristic of their faith is an orientation towards the pursuit of personal holiness. These young people have heard the call of their favourite Pope, St John Paul II, who urged them to become the saints of the new Millennium. His words continue to echo in their hearts:

> Young people of every continent, do not be afraid to be the saints of the new millennium! Be contemplative, love prayer; be coherent with your faith and generous in the service of your brothers and sisters, be active members of the Church and builders of peace. To succeed in this demanding project of life, continue to listen to His Word, draw strength from the Sacraments, especially the Eucharist and Penance. The Lord wants you to be intrepid apostles of his Gospel and builders of a new humanity. (Message to Youth, World Youth Day 2000)

St John Paul II's World Youth Day messages continue to stir the hearts of young people. They know his words are an authentic call and are a real possibility. They want to be saints and so they set out to be holy.

When they think of holiness they understand that it means giving primacy to prayer. Here they do not mean occasional short prayers, but deep and devoted prayer, specifically, silent prayer before the Blessed Sacrament. Indeed, many young people have had a profound experience of knowing the presence of the Lord as they have knelt in silent adoration. They have come to know of His love for them personally as they knelt for long periods in His presence. They felt His love for them as something real and indeed transforming. These young people are drawn with a deeper longing to taste this love and to live under this love. They want the whole Church to discover what they have discovered.

They want the Church to give primacy to prayer because of their own experience. They urge Catholics to embrace prayer before the Blessed Sacrament in the conviction that such prayer will help us live holy lives and help the Church and its leaders to be faithful to its vision and mission. They firmly believe that it is prayer that will reinvigorate the Church and empower its mission.

These young people long for the Church, in its human dimension, to become holy.

Their heartfelt desire is that the celebration of the Sacred Liturgy be a time of worship of God. They want to encounter the Transcendent One every time they go to Mass. They do not need to be attracted to Mass by gimmicks or superficial efforts to appeal to them. They want periods of silence and prayerfulness to be a feature of the Liturgy and genuine worship of God to be the mark of the way in which the liturgy is celebrated.

They don't want many words, banalities and superficial commentary in the Liturgy. They hope that the music will be prayerful, beautiful and directed to the honour of God. They have in their hearts a desire to offer God their praise and thanksgiving. At every Mass they long for a personal and "holy communion" with Jesus their Lord who they know is alive and comes to them when they receive the Body of Christ.

These young Catholics love the Blessed Virgin Mary. She is their spiritual mother. Some express their Marian devotion by saying "Loving Jesus with the heart of Mary". They say the Rosary regularly. They love its simple repetition and see in it a mode for quiet contemplation of divine mysteries. They wear a scapular or a medal of the Virgin Mary, invoking her maternal love and care. They are unafraid to show their devotion to the Mother of God.

They love the saints. They read lives of the saints. They are inspired by their virtue, their faith, their heroism. They have their favourites to whom they pray. The saints are their friends, their companions on the road. They surround themselves with this cloud of witnesses. They are drawn to the youthful saints, saints like Pier Georgio Frasatti, Maria Goretti, Thérèse of Lisieux, Chiara Badano, Philomena, José Sanchez, Francesco and Jacinta Marto, and many others often not known to older Catholics.

They invoke the angels. They pray to their Guardian Angel. They seek the protection of St Michael the Archangel against the powers of darkness. They know that the Christian life is a spiritual warfare. They know that the angels are their spiritual companions.

They have come to appreciate the importance of regular confession. In their desire for holiness they are willing to address the areas of sin in their lives. They know that this sacrament not only frees them from the burden of their sins, but provides grace to enable them to grow in virtue.

These young people have a thirst for a deeper knowledge of the faith. They read sound literature explaining the faith. They attend lectures and seminars. They scour the internet for sound and inspiring material on the Catholic faith. They have a sense of what is wholesome and nourishing and what is counterfeit.

They have a missionary zeal. They are not afraid to declare what they believe. They try to convince their friends, inviting them to Mass, or a talk, or a Catholic event.

A new generation of devout Catholics is rising up. Their number is growing. They are scattered across the nation, now in their thousands. This is a source of hope for the future of the Catholic Church in this nation.

Contribution of the new movements

Much of the renewal of faith among young people has been due to the work of the new ecclesial movements. While a few of the new ecclesial movements have their origins prior to the Second Vatican Council (for example, Opus Dei, Schoenstatt) most movements have their origin in the years after the Council. Across the world, and in Australia, the majority of these new movements have their source in the Charismatic Renewal. From the 1970s the Charismatic Renewal, while initially expressed in the establishing of prayer groups, fostered the formation of various lay-led communities. These communities developed various apostolic works, especially in evangelisation and their particular focus became the evangelisation of young people. These communities developed summer schools, schools of evangelisation and various youth mission teams.

Since the 1980s these various works of evangelisation have touched and changed the lives of thousands of young people. These movements and communities were not only effective agents of evangelisation but also provided programs of formation in the Christian life. One area of importance has been a number of initiatives promoting Catholic teaching on sexuality and marriage, often inspired by St John Paul II's "Theology of the Body".

Vocations to priesthood and religious life

After a significant drought in vocations over recent decades there are signs of a new culture of vocations emerging, particularly to the diocesan priesthood. There are now increasing numbers of young men presenting themselves for the priesthood. They sense not only a vocation to priestly life, but more importantly they have a strong sense of mission. They can see the state of things in the Church and they want to contribute to its future. They want to foster reverent celebration of the Mass and sacraments. They have a passion to preach the faith in fidelity to the tradition. They have an evangelistic zeal and want to draw others to know and love Jesus Christ.

We are witnessing the first signs of a resurgence in vocations among women to religious life. What attracts them are expressions of religious life that are grounded in solid spirituality, in forms of communal life and mission. They want to express their consecration to the Lord by wearing the religious habit. While numbers are relatively small in Australia there are clear signs of new life budding forth.

Laying sound foundations

Now is the time to lay sound foundations upon which the Church will be able to build in the time ahead. The Church may indeed become smaller. It may not have the prominence in society it once enjoyed. However, what is left will be a purer, humbler and more faithful group of believers.

The Church will consist of men and women of deep personal faith, confident in the love of God for them. They will exhibit a spirit of joy and hope even in the midst of difficulty and uncertainty. They will be small but important lights in a growing darkness. They will be the saints of the present and future Church.

From such communities a new missionary endeavour will be born. When the time is right – the Lord's time – they will go forth as the Apostles went forth from Pentecost, as the monks went forth from their monasteries, as missionaries went forth from Europe in the 19th century, to begin a new springtime of evangelisation.

What is important is that now we build sound foundations. The key foundation for each Catholic is a personal relationship with Jesus Christ. The communities of Christians, especially the parishes, must be united in bonds of mutual love and support and have embraced a missionary orientation. Catholic marriages and families must strive to live as a domestic church. And young people embracing the call to holiness, and among them numbers willing to embrace vocations to priesthood and religious life.

Year of St Joseph

Pope Francis in the Apostolic Letter, *Patris Corde*, With a Father's Heart, has declared a Year of St Joseph, commencing on 8 December 2020 and running over a twelve-month period. It recalls the 150th anniversary of the declaration by Pope Pius IX of St Joseph as Patron of the Universal Church.

The words of proclamation give a setting for Pope Pius IX's decision to proclaim St Joseph as Patron of the Universal Church. In his decree he describes what has moved him: "And now therefore, when in these most troublesome times the Church is beset by enemies on every side, and is weighed down by calamities so heavy that ungodly men assert that the gates of hell have at length prevailed against her". In giving this title to St Joseph the Pope says that he entrusts "himself and all the faithful to the Patriarch St Joseph's most powerful patronage".

As we conclude this reflection on the situation of the Church in the third decade of the third millennium of Christianity, and consider what steps are needed to ensure the future of the Church, we entrust the Church to its patron, St Joseph.

Plenary Council and the future of the Church

The Plenary Council is clearly an important moment for the Church in Australia. It can be a moment in which the Church sees its mission clearly, or in can be a moment in which we become confused or distracted with secondary issues. It can be a moment of grace, or a moment of wilful human weakness. It can be a moment when a new course is set that produces rich fruit, or it can be a lost moment from which nothing lasting emerges.

At this Plenary Council we need to lay sound foundations upon which future generations will be able to build. We cannot but pray for the grace of the Holy Spirit to come upon us as we meet to discern the future path for the Church in Australia.

> Mary, Help of Christians, Patroness of Australia, pray for us.
> St Joseph, Patron of the Universal Church, pray for us.

www.ingramcontent.com/pod-product-compliance
Lightning Source LLC
Chambersburg PA
CBHW032302150426
43195CB00008BA/549